AT THE COURT OF KOREA

At the Court of Korea is a compelling blend of travel and international politics in the Far East. Selected when very young for the US Foreign Service, Sands was first sent to Japan in the early 1890s. Having learnt Japanese and studied Japan's national characteristics in some detail, he was then transferred to Korea where he proceeded to become the main adviser to the king, and remained so until his dramatic ousting two years later. It was while in Korea that Sands wrote these 'Undiplomatic Memories', a most revealing and perspicacious analysis of a changing country at the turn of the century.

This edition includes an introduction by Christopher Hitchens, author of *The Elgin Marbles* (Chatto & Windus, 1987), putting *At the Court of Korea* into a modern perspective and relating Sands's experiences of the country to the Korea of today.

D1513733

The cover shows 'A Military Encampment Outside a Walled City' (Martin Gregory)

AT THE
COURT OF KOREA

Undiplomatic Memories

William Franklin Sands

WITH AN INTRODUCTION by
CHRISTOPHER HITCHENS

CENTURY
London   Melbourne   Auckland   Johannesburg

© Introduction Christopher Hitchens 1987

This edition first published in 1987 by Century,
an imprint of Century Hutchinson Ltd, Brookmount House,
62–65 Chandos Place, London WC2N 4NW

Century Hutchinson Australia Pty Ltd,
PO Box 496, 16–22 Church Street, Hawthorn,
Victoria 3122, Australia

Century Hutchinson New Zealand Limited
PO Box 40-086, Glenfield, Auckland 10, New Zealand

Century Hutchinson South Africa (Pty) Ltd
PO Box 337, Berglvei, 2012 South Africa

Typeset in Garamond by BookEns, Saffron Walden
Printed and bound in Great Britain
by Richard Clay Ltd, Bungay

ISBN 0 7126 1765 5

The publishers regret that they have been unable to reproduce the original
illustrations in this edition. We would like to apologise for any inconvenience
this might cause.

CONTENTS

INTRODUCTION

'THE East', said Disraeli in one of his grandiloquent moments, 'is a career'. One sees what he must have meant. All kinds of literary and political examples appear to amplify his point. James Mill laboured for years on his vast *History of British India* without visiting the subcontinent and without mastering any of its languages. Others spent their lives in Asia only to compose memoirs of tremendous banality and condescension. The fact that many Europeans saw and found 'the Orient' as a possession has also to be allowed for. The most successful and penetrating analysts and *raconteurs* were often those, like Lafcadio Hearn, who were without fixed national allegiance.

So that *At the Court of Korea*, by William Franklin Sands, is the more extraordinary as a book and as a 'find'. It is not a dispassionate book. It has the right mixture of the objective and the committed. Both the time and the man favoured this lucky outcome. Sands was an American professional who came to Asia without preconceptions and who hoped to make Korea his 'career' in an age when America and empire were not yet synonymous. His memoir is an intriguing account of a country, and a haunting record of a disappointment.

The American engagement with the Korean peninsula has been episodic; varying and fluctuating between the convulsive and the neglectful. There is still no national memorial, for instance, to the thousands of United States servicemen who never returned from the Korean War. Yet at one time that conflict eclipsed all other domestic and foreign considerations. It was the first commitment of American forces on the Asian mainland (if one discounts Second World War 'advisers') and very nearly the last. It almost led to a nuclear war, and just stopped short of an invasion of China. It provided a classic test, in Washington, of will and nerve between civilian and military authority. Today, although the commander of the South Korea armed forces is an American general, and although American arms remain in the country at some strength and on permanent alert, the attention paid by the public and by the press and politicians is intermittent and slight. Occasional dramas, such as the attempt of the South Korean authorities to purchase Congressmen in the late 1970s, or the Soviet destruction of Korean Airlines Flight 007, illuminate a special relationship between the two countries. But, as I said, interest is fitful and real concern is rare.

The United States shed blood in and for Korea, between 1950 and 1953, under the nominal flag of the United Nations, which may help to explain absence of a collective memory and the reluctance of Americans to think of Korea as their responsibility. When William Franklin Sands first set foot in the country just before the turn of the last century, Korea was also object of a concert, or concerts, of powers. The expansion of imperial Japan was a growing threat to the whole of the neighbouring littoral, and this gave the rival emperor in Russia an additional spur to pursue a 'window on the East' and a maritime outlet south of Vladivostock. The European powers, principally England, France and Germany, tended towards the Japanese. The United States kept up an affectation of neutrality. It was only on the verge of its 'mission' as a Pacific power, and had made no apparently binding commitments or alliances.

There could hardly have been more scope and latitude, then, for a young and energetic American diplomat. William Franklin Sands was, by nature, struck more from the adventurer's than from the bureaucratic or proconsular mould. He was a gallant, optimistic harbinger of 'the American century'. Well and roundly educated, confident, and equipped with good Washington and family connections, he could represent the New World at its most sprightly and genuine. It was intended, by the White House and the State Department, that he should be part of a new breed and generation of diplomats. He was to be allowed to take his time, to acquaint himself with new languages and peoples, to immerse himself in the habits and culture of the East. As the initial chapters of *At the Court of Korea* show, Sands had no difficulty in taking these directions. He succeeded, with great charm and address, in making himself trusted. One has to remember that Korea had been almost hermetically sealed from the outside world for centuries; its rulers and inhabitants long used to making its exterior seem minatory and its interior too hot for foreigners.

> The coasts were made as uninviting as possible to discourage strangers, and in the interior whole forests were burned off centuries ago, and the hills kept bare until the top soil had washed down, in order to discourage tigers.

The doors of 'the Hermit Kingdom' were opened to the outside even later than those of Japan, and much more tentatively. So for Sands to be asked to become counsellor of the Korean royal household, at the age of twenty-five and after only a few years in the country, was an unprecedented mark of acceptance. And that was the position in which he found himself in the year of grace 1900.

Sands's political and diplomatic master was John Hay, the Secretary of State. The very name Hay is coterminous with the 'Open Door'; the policy which he successfully imposed on China after the Boxer Rising. Under Presidents McKinley and Roosevelt, Hay worked assiduously but not too ostentatiously at securing and expanding American power overseas. Having been a private secretary to Abraham Lincoln and an unusually Anglophile ambassador to London, he was no stranger to politics. But he liked also to be thought of as a poet, a stylist and a phrase-maker. His long friendship with Henry Adams shows how well he succeeded in both ambitions. T. S. Eliot in his 1919 review of Henry Adams's *Education*, spoke without evident irony of:

> The great John Hay, who had been engaged in settling the problems of China and Cuba and Manchuria.

Hay himself felt that there was a 'cosmic tendency' leading America to expand. 'The briefest expression of our rule of conduct,' he wrote 'is, perhaps, the Monroe Doctrine and the Golden Rule. With this simple chart we can hardly go wrong.' Privately, he could be, and was, more feline. In 1898 he wrote from the Court of St James to Theodore Roosevelt, setting down his congratulations on the American humiliation of Spain, and her effortless acquisition of Cuba and the Philippines:

> It has been a splendid little war; begun with the highest motives, carried on with magnificence and spirit, favored by that Fortune which loves the brave. It is now to be concluded, I hope, with that fine good nature which is, after all, the distinguishing trait of the American character.

Later scholars have read this as a coded counsel of restraint and a warning against imperial *hubris*, which it may well have been. But Hay was eager to serve the imperialist Roosevelt in a high capacity, and chose not to mince words when addressing Sands. He had to relinquish him as an envoy when he took up his duties as adviser to the Emperor of Korea. But he had by no means lost him as an agent, and wrote to him in these terms:

> You will have a most interesting experience and you may and ought to derive from it something of considerable value to our government when and *if*, you return. There is an 'if'. You have a very good chance not to return undamaged. You have only one complete certainty – that is that the govern-

ment of the United States will not under any circumstance be drawn into any complications which may arise out of your troubles. You do not represent the United States or American influence in any way. You are an adventurer as far as we are concerned. When you have lived out your contract (if you do) it is logical to expect that the then Secretary of State will make use of a unique experience and take you back into service.

Sands appears to have been happy to take this advice literally. In his dealings with the sinuous and ruthless Prince Ito, head of the Japanese legation in Seoul, he contrived to act as if he were his own man. (So much so, in fact, that when the game was over Prince Ito vainly offered him a post in the Japanese puppet administration.) Sands's diagnosis, made at the end of his book, was that American 'neutrality' towards Korea had only facilitated the Japanese take-over of the country, and that a refusal to risk American life or reputation had thrown away a great potential prize. He seems to have been naïve in making this judgement, as even the toughest field operators often are. Prince Ito had his counterpart in Washington, in the shape of the Japanese minister Baron Kogoro Takahira. After Japan had decisively humbled the Russians on sea and land in 1904 – events which Sands witnessed with his own eyes – the Baron paid a call on John Hay. He asked him to urge all powers to permit Japan to maximize her post-war gains. Hay agreed to this while keeping up his public stance of neutrality. He died on 1 July 1905 (Henry Adams learned the news 'as he was strolling down to dine under the trees at Armenonville') and his successor Elihu Root took his duplicitous policy to its consummation. The Root-Takahira Executive Agreement, concluded in 1908, gave Japan a free hand along the Pacific seaboard and helped create the force which the United States would one day, have to fight to the death. Sands, in fact, had been exerting himself for nothing.

This last judgement may seem unfair. But it appears to be warranted by his own concluding chapter, which recounts how on his return to Washington:

> The State Department was not interested either. Everybody there, including all who had never been in the East knew so much more than I did that I felt very small, and decided never to speak of it again.

Teddy Roosevelt, too, had been deaf to his reports. The *finale* of the book has Sands being sent off to help with one of John Hay's other great schemes – the establishment of American control over a canal to be cut through the Central American isthmus. At that stage, it had not been decided whether to dig it through Panama or Nicaragua . . . .

Obviously it is too harsh to say that Sands wasted his time in Korea. In spite of the cynicism of his own government and the unscrupulous opposition of the Japanese faction, he made a sincere attempt to inculcate a reformist spirit in the country. His personal statement of aims still reads very well:

> I had some influence with the emperor; he listened to me with confidence. I also knew that there was a considerable body of Korean officials who would prefer to be honest and were as decent as the system let them be. Several powerful nobles were heartily ashamed of the backwardness of their country and might be expected to help in a reform programme. I counted on the American party in the palace to become the chief advocates for reform, and on the American mission-trained natives and the oppressed peasants to support it enthusiastically.

Sands here is the forerunner of the Peace Corps generation, of the numberless Americans, quiet and otherwise, who have laboured in good faith to restrain some despot or persuade some client; to keep him sweet while teaching him the merits of land reform, purified water and an independent civil service. Too often, these 'advisers' have ended up like the character described by Sands, 'Colonel' Ninstead. 'No one knew what his functions were in the Korean government, though he wore their military uniform. Probably he did not either. He had been a pay clerk in the American navy and perhaps fancied himself paymaster-general of the unpaid imperial forces.' We have all met Ninstead.

Indeed, Sands is surprisingly contemporary, throughout his book, in his reflections. He states boldly that, 'As far as consular courts in Eastern Asia are concerned, that war into which England was forced by opium bootleggers, and which led to all our treaties with China, showed plainly enough the danger of allowing large numbers of foreigners to live in countries where they could not in justice be submitted to native law.' Scholars as conservative as Bernard Lewis have dated the start of the Iranian revolution from the day in October 1964 when the Shah's parliament was persuaded to grant 'extraterritorial' rights to Americans living in the country.

A little later, Sands adds the strikingly modern thought that, 'when Europe, after centuries of development, came back into contact with Asia on the far side of the world, all that ancient arrogance, tinged with ancient fear, flamed to life again; only, instead of Carl Martel's hammer or the Crusader's emblems, this time the people of the West carried national prestige and commerce on their banners.' Sands makes it clear that the United States did not, in this respect, learn from the mistakes of its European predecessors.

Japan, of course, went in early for promiscuous borrowing of European methods and attitudes: quickly acquiring her own sense of a 'civilising mission' and compounding new techniques with ancient feelings of apartness and superiority. Sands saw and felt the strivings of this new imperialism – what might he have said if he had known of the urbane Hay and his deft but short-sighted compromise with it?

I've felt bound to stress the politics of Sands's book; the practice of statecraft as it appeared to him and as it now appears to us. But his memoir should also be read for the pleasure it affords. To really know and love another country and another people is a privilege given to fairly few people and to depressingly few diplomats. Sands had this privilege. During his brief time in Japan – his first posting in Asia – he had read and appreciated the newly published works of Lafcadio Hearn, the Greek-Irish romantic who set himself to *become* Japanese before 'interpreting' the country to others. Sands may have been struck by Hearn's emphasis on *Kokoro* – 'the heart of things'. And, like Hearn, he was able to look about him and to see the Koreans without romance but without bigotry or stereotype. His chapters on custom, on friendship and on religion are illuminating and sometimes touching. He was concerned, as he wrote, not to 'Americanise' the country, but to give it the chance to see and try alternatives without coercion. He was careful of local susceptibilities; being very circumspect (in another oddly contemporary allusion) about the enclosed and xenophobic city of Peng Yang, today the seat of Kim Il Sung's grotesque cultist regime. Korea was and is a febrile country, poorly braced for the shock of the new. It could have been very lucky in its first encounter with an enlightened scion of the New World. It was not Sands's fault that this initial meeting should have turned into a puzzle and then a trick. He knew that the Koreans hoped for American support, not merely the support of an American. He never became immodest about the reasons for his preferment. So much greater, then, the disappointment at the waste of his vigour and goodwill.

Elihu Root later told Sands that, 'I could never be a diplomat if I tried with both hands, according to the

Department's concept of the diplomat; for I had learned to do things on my own judgement and to fight my way through all obstacles and guard my own head, which does not make a good secretary.' How right, in his own narrow terms, Root has turned out to be. The Sands tradition has quite died out, and the age of conformists, spooks, fixers and placemen seems to have been with us for ever. In a brilliant essay on American diplomacy ('Imperialism without Splendor') published in 1982, the Lebanese scholar Fouad Ajami wrote of the British colonial mavericks such as T. E. Lawrence, Gertrude Bell and H. St John Philby that theirs

> may have been a doomed affair, an empire acquired when the tide had turned against empire. But even at the moment of its dissolution, Pax Britannica imposed on its governors the burden of encountering the lives of others, of travelling into their poetry and language, of getting under their skin.

Ajami may be overpraising the British for purposes of counterpoint, but it's difficult to dissent from his picture of Pax Americana, where

> the life and reality of another society are appropriated, turned into echoes of what will be said and written 'in Washington'. No need for intellectual toil; no need to traverse forbidding deserts, as Philby and Bell did; no need to take the sensibilities and dilemmas of another culture on their own terms. From Washington one can survey the entire scene, self-importantly proclaiming that the future of another society will be determined in one's own capital.

Indeed, the East is a career. As Ajami puts it:

> Clearly, there are limits to how far societies with deeply different sensibilities can 'walk' with one another. Were we to understand these limits, we would tread more carefully. We would leave it to others to determine their own priorities; we would know when the limits were being violated, and then we would back off and refrain from asking others to join our crusades while we slight their concerns. It is difficult to do –

it means we need, as Clifford Geertz has put it, 'to come to terms with the lives and thoughts of strangers.'

As I re-read that passage, I thought of Sands sleeping 'for weeks with a pistol in one hand and a Japanese sword in the other' and of his long rides into the interior. I also thought of his pal, the Governor Ye, who had been a true friend in numerous court intrigues, and who was devoted to the idea of Korea's independence. He called Sands to his bedside one night and was found to be 'fearfully swollen and hardly able to speak, but still gay and laughing. I offered to send at once for a foreign doctor.' The Governor needed no telling that he had been lethally poisoned by a rival.

'Yes,' he chuckled, 'I ought to have known better, an old bird like me. It doesn't matter. We can't save the country. Save my son for old friendship's sake, for I really have been your friend.' And he smiled at me and died.

Sands is no fatalist, but he is capable of *rapport* with someone who is. This small achievement would be impossible without a long and sincere absorption in the life of the country. True, the Chief Eunuch had lived in Washington and was able to supply *rapport* from the other direction. But, in the post-Sands generations of American diplomacy, many well-intended gestures have been rudely misinterpreted, and many priceless opportunities chucked away.

Korea has been one of this century's sorriest losers in the game of nations. The brutal Japanese conquest and occupation was followed by a grim and protracted war, which left the country riven and destitute. The Cold War succeeded the Second World War with barely a remission, and Korea became the site of a terrifying conflict between the superpowers. This was ended by an iron partition, which followed a geographical parallel rather than any national or political contour. Today, the northern portion of the country is ruled by one of the most exorbitant despotisms of all time; a hysterical cult of personality accompanied by its natural counterpart, the total subordination of the individual. To the south, we find a classic authoritarian dictatorship, resting upon a military caste, American aid, monopolies, cheap labour and the patronage of certain opportunist foreign 'concessions'.

There is one man who embodies opposition to both these varieties of tyranny, and who expresses the simultaneous aspirations for reunification and for democratic self-government. Having suffered under the North Koreans during the war, Kim Dae Jung has endured a decade and a half of imprisonment and exile for his convictions, ever since he garnered 46 per cent of the South Korean vote in a badly-rigged election in 1971. He has been kidnapped, he has been severely injured in an assassination attempt, and he has been sentenced to death. Between 1982 and 1985 he lived in exile in the United States, and while I was writing this introduction I decided to go and see him. I found a man who deserves that strange title 'tempered by suffering' but whose commitment to his principles is as adamant as ever.

Like all those who believe in a free and independent Korea, Kim has an ambivalent attitude to the United States. His dilemma is not unlike that of those who put their faith in Sands – he wants both more and less American intervention. That's to say, he resents American support for the dismal regime in his country, he wishes Korea to be self-determining, and he knows that American help will be needed to bring that outcome about. On the very day we met, he had taken the risky decision to return to Seoul where he faced renewed imprisonment and persecution, because he had lost hope in effecting a change in American policy by living in Washington and reasoning with Ronald Reagan's State Department.

As we concluded our conversation, Kim drew a sheet of

paper towards him and began writing in Korean characters with an exquisite brush pen. The characters were Speech-Road-Open-Closed-Rise-Fall(Be)-Related. Together, they formed a maxim of Lee Yul Kok, who had been a prominent scholar and politician under the Yi dynasty, to the effect that, 'Whether a nation allows freedom of expression to flourish determines whether it prospers or founders.' The paper was given to me, with a dedication, as a keepsake. I felt moved to ask Kim whether he had ever heard of the American William Franklin Sands. He said he regretted that he had not. So I promised to send him a copy of *At the Court of Korea*, to read on his long ride home.

Christopher Hitchens
Washington D.C.

PROLOGUE: UPON DIPLOMACY

THESE memories of the early days of a 'career' diplomat are, perhaps, incomplete without some explanatory comment upon career diplomacy in general and American diplomatic practice in particular. It is generally accepted to-day that American career foreign service started with Roosevelt; quite probably because there is nobody left in the diplomatic service who started there earlier than the Roosevelt administration. Veterans are not encouraged.

As a matter of fact the career service actually antedates Roosevelt. It had been felt that too many juniors in diplomacy were wealthy young men wanting posts at European courts for the sole purpose of making acquaintance there which would advance them socially at home, and that much reasonably good material was being spoiled in the process with no satisfactory results for anybody. They believed it scarcely possible to send an impressionable youth to a court in Europe and have him come out unaffected by the point of view of the golden gentlemen around whom it centred. They decided to pick a few youngsters whom they knew, and to send them first to the Pacific, either to the South American capitals or to the Far East, to study the working of concession diplomacy, spheres of influence and dollar diplomacy generally, away from the attractions of courts; to watch European diplomacy in the raw, in the regions where presently American interests would be greatly affected. After service there, these first career diplomats were to come home and take a special course at some good

American college supplementary to what they had been seeing, mainly in history and economics. They were to study America from their new point of view and get a sound interpretation of what American interests really are. Then they were to go through a clerkship in the State Department and learn not only the routine of the Department itself, but the manner of working of the whole American system of government. Only after that were they to be permitted to go to Europe, and only the most tried and reliable of them then.

There was no particular reason why I should be appointed to be the first of these, except that both the President and the Secretary of State were friends of my father, and that I had several European languages to begin with and had matriculated for university in Europe.

I had felt frightfully important, of course, and when I was given the choice between first secretary in Chile and second secretary at the legation in Tokyo, I chose the latter, in order to 'finish' Asia, work back to South America and then display my accumulated wisdom and experience in Europe. I was not yet twenty-one years old when I was appointed, and had to wait before my commission could be legal.

It seemed to me quite natural then that a President and a Secretary of State should take the trouble to explain to me exactly what they wanted and why they wanted it. I felt that it was hardly respectable not to be on easy terms with Presidents and Secretaries of State.

Had not Presidents, from Grant on, been frequent and informal visitors in my grandfather's house (except Chester Arthur, who was not approved of, and not received)?

Even the complete lack of interest in my existence of everybody in the State Department except the Secretary did not shake my serene confidence. 'The department,' in those days, consisted of a close corporation within the Department; of a Secretary of State who in the eyes of the inner circle was an outsider and was expected to be an unreliable and possibly a dangerous person, to be watched and thwarted if necessary, and two bodies of 'public enemies' – the diplomatic service and the consular body. Both these latter bodies were usually made up of political appointees, like postmasters at home. They were not expected by the departmental family to last long, nor to do anything worth the trouble of doing while in office. The main hope of the inner departmental circle was that 'lame ducks' would do nothing too preposterous before they vanished into the outer darkness to be replaced by other lame ducks.

Flaming youth of twenty years made a mental note, during the statutory thirty days' period of instruction, to undertake considerable reform in the Department after salvaging the Far East. He never got around to that, however.

My own foreign service covers a period of transition in the diplomatic service, but, living continually on the firing line where immediate action was often necessary, without available precedent or anyone to consult before acting, that experience was very different from the well-ordered routine of diplomatic life to-day. It is the personal experience of those early years that I have sketched here.

CHAPTER 1

JAPAN

JAPAN, thirty-five years ago, like Greece in the 'forties was a subject on which anyone might try his poetic wings. The poetry was there, even if one were not quite conscious of what it meant. The most stolid silk or tea merchant could not wholly escape the subtle witchery of its romance. Even the perfectly green American second secretary of legation that I was could not escape it, nor was it a mere matter of twenty years and golden youth. Everywhere about lay a mystery that either lured or irritated, but one felt it and could not escape. The Japanese themselves, the islands in which they lived, their customs and their language seemed so utterly unlike anything ever imagined that either they absorbed the stranger in an attempt to understand, or he rejected it as impossible to understand; though when Japan approximated the ways and manners of the West, the transition brought some vague disappointment, even to those who did not like them, as of something lost.

There was nothing, anywhere, quite like a Japanese landscape, whether in cherry or azalea season, chrysanthemums, lotus or red maples, or in plain winter garb. The mountains do show up jagged and in fantastic shapes, just as they do in the Japanese prints and kakemono; there is a quality in the atmosphere, particularly in early morning, which plays all the strange tricks with perspective that seem so unreal and impossible in Japanese art. The broken volcanic background is really softened by blending of bamboo and conifers in the same curious way that is so characteristic of their painting, and Fuji really looks like that and is never twice the same. The peasant, knee-deep in the black mud of the rice fields, worked in the same way, with the same implements as the peasant did thousands of years before him, and still looked with curiosity at the arrogant Western 'barbarian' riding along the narrow dike that separated the wet fields. The peasant, unconscious that the barbarian was nothing more formidable than a wondering American school-boy suddenly projected into official life, marvelled, no doubt, why the foreigner was not subject to that old rule of Japanese life which permitted a warrior to cut down any man who behaved to him in an 'unexpected' manner. Unexpected, in Japanese, was the word we use for rude or discourteous, courtesy being expected in every branch of life and every age: the slightest departure from the strict ritual and ceremonial of Japanese life was unexpected, therefore discourteous. Strict adherence to the ritual gave to Japanese daily life the appearance of a well-rehearsed pageant, in which every act was carefully thought out and perfectly performed, though European 'unexpectedness' and the use of machinery were beginning to jar the smooth flow of the procession. On the rare occasions when the peasant came to town, or when he used the steam cars to make his distant pilgrimages to some holy spot or place of special beauty, he still left his sandals on the train platform before taking his place in the car, for the Japanese does not bring his dirty shoes into a room and a railway carriage was only a moving room.

In town, natives and foreigners alike rode in rickshaws, the light two-wheeled vehicle hardly bigger in body than a baby carriage. If it was a private conveyance it was drawn by two swift runners in the livery of the owner's house, bearing monogram or crest upon the runners' shirts as well as upon the car itself. If one used a horse, a liveried betto or running groom sped through the streets ahead of his master, warning pedestrians to give place. During the daytime throngs of men and women dressed in soft silks or cottons, and working men with no dress but a loin cloth or over it the short jacket of the mechanic, filled the streets with the murmur of polite exchange of conversational ritual; with the soft padding of bare feet or the rhythmical scrape of high wooden pattens whose two supports of thin hard wood were tuned to a musical accord. At night the streets were empty and the silence unbroken, except in summer by the myriads of insects whose shrilling is an age-old theme in Japanese poems. High over the wide sea of low roofs, tiled or thatched, fire watchmen perched on flimsy scaffold towers, to signal the direction of danger from the terrific conflagrations caused by some carelessness in the dry wooden houses, which were a constant menace. Often at night a murmur would arise in the whole silent area – at first a dull whisper of human voices awakening from sleep, then sharp exclamations of fear and warning, as the tremor of an earthquake swept over the city.

The foreigner might live, if he wished, in a Japanese house, built of choice woods delicately tinted, roofed high with soft grey tiles swinging out in graceful curves to the pointed corner eaves; the floors built of soft, padded white straw mats, the inner partitions of opaque paper panels, which run back in sliding grooves of wood, opening enchanting vistas through the whole house of close garden or wide park, with some century-old conifer shading the narrow polished veranda. He might live as I did, overlooking the Temple of the Forty-seven Ronin, those 'masterless men,' paragons of Japanese knightly loyalty, whose story is one of the great Japanese classics. When, in the stillness of an autumn night, some lady sheltered behind her garden walls sang the old poems of Japan to the music of her harp, he might watch the mossy tombstones of the Ronin, half expecting to see their armoured figures in the moonlight. Indeed, even that

sight was not impossible. I actually did meet a group of
knights, returning home one night through the great
temple park. In full armour they were, each with his two
swords, helmeted and with visors raised over grim faces,
showing that however accustomed these men might be to
the frock coat and silk hat of Europe, the trappings of the
feudal samurai were still their natural dress. They were
clansmen making the immemorial New Year's visit of
allegiance to their former chieftain, despite railroads and
banks, telephones, parliaments and new political parties.

Many have tried their hand at a bit of fine writing about
Japan, but very few have caught or can convey to others
the crowding impressions that streamed in on any open
mind in those days before Japan went industrial.

Only Lafcadio Hearn has really caught it. Certainly no
one has expressed it as he does. Perhaps his insight had to
do with some Celtic mysticism hidden in his Irish soldier
father; the British army has fostered some queer things,
as anyone knows who knows his Kipling. Perhaps he drew
it from the springs of some ancient Hellenic paganism in
his Greek island mother. From whatever source, he felt
Japan, and Hellas was all about. One could hardly go
along the sea-shore remote from the haunts of the outport foreign colonies, or stop in some hidden village off
the travelled highways, without a vision, as in a flash of
light, of what must have been Greek rustic life and customs in the Golden Age. Through all the simple life away
from the cities, through all the common view of life of
humble people ran a revelation of our own older world.
The gentle contact of the older Irish with spiritual things,
the deification of all nature in ancient rural Greece were
both part of Japan.

It was just the lack of that Celtic-Greek sense of the
spirit world and of spiritual values which kept Pierre Loti
from any conception of Japan. He has done good
landscape sketching in words, but his thoughts in Japan,
as they were in Constantinople, are always on fleeting
sentimental adventures.

Loti does not even approach the spirit of Japan, the Soul. Yet there is a soul, and it was not hidden except by accidental veils. It filled and quickened every member of the body of Japan, as is the nature of the soul.

One's own strangeness and foreignness was the real obstacle to understanding, and one could not know the new Japan without knowing the soul and body underneath the new European forms. It was impossible not to feel one's self really something uncouth and awkward among people who are naturally gracious and graceful. No one has ever seen an awkward Japanese of the old school, in his own setting.

The presence of a stranger from overseas in any primitive spot of the inner country was an immediate damper upon all ordinary life. The language was a barrier, no easier to cross through the medium of English spoken by a native, for they were self-conscious and reticent about themselves and their customs, as indeed they had learned to be in face of Western obtuseness. It was only when simple folk had become used to him, when gradually the spirit and poetry of a very difficult tongue began to take form, and he could overcome their natural shyness by friendly intercourse, that a foreigner might come and go among them without disturbing their lives, and his halting efforts to talk ceased to be a bar before an innate courtesy which tried to understand rather than to ridicule.

The real barrier did not seem to me to be any difference of race, or to lie in the facile maxim that 'East is East and West is West, and never the twain shall meet.' It seemed rather to grow from ourselves and the great distance we had come from our own lives in the beginnings of Europe. It seemed unpardonable to me not to see that so many of those things which appeared to be so contrary to all our experience were not really so; that many of them were very much our own, only that we had discarded and forgotten the experience of our own past. Perhaps, in Americans, one might grant it as natural after all, but not in Europeans. European society, up to less than four hundred years ago, was built upon Christian chivalry, and European civilization derived from that time when Europe was Roman and Greek.

One could not be long in contact with Japanese life without consciousness of the reality of 'bushido,' the code of honour of the warrier. It seemed fantastic to the ultra-modern Westerner only because he had forgotten or never heard of the ideal Christian knighthood, 'the broad stone of honour' upon which European customs were based. We were puzzled by the apparent inconsistencies between the rigidity of this code and the petty difficulties which constantly arose in the mercantile world, forgetting that as in earlier Europe, Japanese society had grown up about the man of the sword, the poet and the agriculturist, and that trading had been left to a despised class of city dwellers, a bourgeoisie, of whom honour and chivalry were not expected.

Bushido was the training of the man of the sword. It held something of Roman austerity, something of the character-forming discipline of the Roman in his old best days; and it held much also of the Christian discipline placed by a religion of peace upon the wild and barbarian fighting clansmen of Gothic Europe, to form of him the 'perfect gentle knight.'

Bushido and all the life that centred around it should have been immediately intelligible to any Spaniard, in terms of 'hidalguia,' that all-compelling sense of caste of the noble of Spain emanating from him and forming the character also of the Spanish peasant, both men of the soil. It should have been equally clear to the most Prussian of *Junkers*.

All these older things in our racial lives have gone so completely from our memory, however, that Japan seemed hopelessly unknowable, as though we had passed literally through Alice's looking-glass and into a beautiful garden where we looked at everything in reverse.

The diplomatic corps, rather haughtily aloof from the

business world of Yokohama and the outports, was
occupied with appraisal of the real strength of this new
nation, with its ability to assimilate a European form,
with the possibility of danger, should Japan become a
power, to that jealousy of national prestige which was the
motive force behind a diplomacy only gradually sup-
planting the old dynastic rivalries and feuds of Europe –
not yet sure of its modern direction.

Our dean, Sir Ernest Satow, was feared by his own people
though kindness itself to me. Quite likely he saw in me
another unsophisticated infant such as he was himself
when he came out in 1862. I stood second in rank below
the American minister himself, and if anything happened
to him and to the first secretary, I would be in charge of
American interests in the Japanese Empire, which was
growing rapidly to be one of the four great world powers.
The only safety in that situation lay in the experience and
great tact of Ransford Miller, labelled the 'Japanese' secretary because he read, spoke and wrote Japanese, but
under our system he was out of line at that time for promotion, though he was the only one of us who knew
fluently the language in which our business was conducted.
For whatever reason, Sir Ernest always treated me differently from the other fledgelings of the diplomatic
corps. He had come out thirty-four years before, and in a
similar way. He had gained his experience at first-hand
and was using it with wisdom.

Even though in 1862, before the restoration of the
emperor, the legations were at private war with the
unruly clans, and the cutting down of some foreigner
upon the highway was almost of daily occurrence, the
gay-hearted lad of nineteen that Sir Ernest was must have
caught something of the secret of Japan. Those years
formed a background of distrust in most old timers. For
Sir Ernest they were years of romance and adventure.
When he came to publish his book, however, fifty-nine
years later, it was with the political life and growth of new

Japan that he dealt, with as slender an account as possible of his own share therein. Forgotten or sealed in the statesman's heart were the memories of a reckless boy who broke bounds in spite of danger and of official displeasure; who learned really to know Japan, and formed those lifelong friendships with Japanese boys of his own age which made him a power in diplomacy when they became the elder statesmen and controlled the building of a new world power out of the remnants of the suppressed clans.

The Russian minister, M. Hitrovo, could not be expected to know anything about the country nor to want to learn. He had been transferred hastily to Tokyo from a Balkan capital where the wholesale assassination of a government had been brought too close to his legation for comfort.

The French legation, even though it had some excellent men, civilian and military, was merely a string to Russia's fiddle and everybody knew it. France, Austria and Italy formed the social centres for the diplomatic set. France's fate was bound with Russia's; Italy watched France and Germany, not Japan. Germany, I think, could hardly have been well informed by Baron von Gutschmid, the eccentric head of an inharmonious legation whose vagaries were cut short by his whipping an imperial cadet in the public street. It is hard to say which was the greater sacrilege: to touch the imperial uniform, or to strike an imperial aspirant officer. In addition, the boy belonged to a noble and powerful family. One would think that von Gutschmid would have known that, for in Prussia there was also noble caste, there was also veneration for the Kaiser's uniform and for the persons of the Kaiser's men-of-war. Utter disregard of similar customs to one's own in other countries was not, however, a monopoly of any individual. It was the fashion for all foreigners. We were looking for differences not likenesses.

Belgium was already becoming synonymous with

Russia and France in the Far East, but the Belgian minister, Baron d'Anethan (or de Nathan as some said his name had been originally) was nobody's man. I should think he was easily the shrewdest diplomat in Tokyo. If anyone saw very far into the future, it would be the kindly, cynical little baron. I never heard of his leaving a diary for publication. It would be interesting. The baroness was a Haggard and a poetess. Her entertainments always had a literary flavour. One brushed one's wits for her affairs. One danced at the French legation.

The most generally liked people in the corps were the Spaniards. Two years later, when we were at war, the members of the Spanish and the American legations conformed rigidly to the etiquette prescribed in a neutral country. When one of them happened to call and found an 'enemy' there, the 'enemy,' as first comer, would rise, bow formally but with scrupulous politeness to the new arrival and take his leave, according to the protocol; but under cover of night the Spaniards, having no news of their own of the progress of the war, would come to the Americans privately, and the Americans, knowing nothing officially, would tell them all they knew from the home papers. Our countries might be at war, but we did not hate, and (since all of those concerned on the American side are dead) I admit some pride in believing that they acted like gentlemen in the matter, though perhaps it was only shirt-sleeves diplomacy.

Our own chief was as far removed from the professional diplomat as is possible to imagine. A great ruddy giant of an Ohio Scot, he had come out to the government experimental farms in the Hokkaido as an agricultural expert. He learned Japanese, of course, and later was appointed first secretary of legation, and then minister. As honest as the sunshine, Edwin Dun enjoyed the confidence of the Japanese government as greatly in his way as Sir Ernest in his. Not that the Japanese told him everything they knew, but I do not think it would have occurred to any of them to finesse with him. They trusted him and he them, which is the best basis yet devised for successful diplomacy, and I know no one who did not like him as a man.

Of my immediate colleagues among the juniors Gerard Lowther of the British legation stands out in affectionate memory for his sterling character, though he was more widely known for his theory about dinners. His little dinners were perfection. Six was the perfect number, four steadies and two strangers, all well chosen; food, wine, tobacco and service of the best, exactly enough – neither too much nor too little – and good conversation. Lowther went later as ambassador to Constantinople. At that time it was probably the one capital in the world where he was utterly and completely out of place. Of the old county stock which, until the World War, governed England by inheritance, unobtrusively but most solidly convinced that there are things an Englishman cannot do, he could no more have understood the young Turk, or made a friend of him, stained with the blood of revolution, than he could have worn tan shoes with full dress. Lowther was never the man to develop the young Turk, but he would have made a first-rate ambassador to Washington or Madrid. There were many men in the East then who have since become famous. Count von Spee and Sir Christopher Cradock, sailors of the same type, the same training and the same tastes, gentlemen both, and good friends, tried out in the World War the theories they used to discuss in Tokyo. Von Spee won, but how it must have hurt him that he did. At the end of 1897 Commodore Dewey, an old friend, was bemoaning his fate that, war with Spain being inevitable, he had been given the Asiatic station where nothing could possibly happen:

'It is indecent to fight Spain anyhow. Now, if France would come in too, we could save our faces, but best of all if Germany would come in. If only Germany could be prevailed on to come in!' Dewey did not foresee Manila Bay.

At one time, also, a French major of artillery stayed with me, a most attractive personality, with whom I corresponded vigorously for several years. He was attached later to General Voyron's staff, then, if I remember correctly, to the staff of an obscure General Joffre whom nobody knew. He was Nivelle of France.

There were men, French, German, English and American, who were studying Japan from many angles, and whose works are pieces of value in that mosaic history of Japan, which, as Sir Ernest Satow says, has not yet been written because we have drawn only on our conflicting observation and not on Japanese contemporary sources. Captain Brinckley, Josiah Conder, Basil Hall Chamberlain, Fenellosa, Dr Baelz (to whom the imperial family owes so much) and a dozen others were making their names known in a new and enchanting field.

Life in Tokyo, or far in the interior, was the golden side. The shadow side was in the ports. Rough manners were not lacking there, nor mutual distrust, nor occasional clashes and outbursts of racial antagonism. One very fruitful source of conflict was the relations of Europeans with Japanese women. Quite too frequently there were exhibitions of partiality on the part of minor officials, where disputes arose between foreigners and their own, and plenty of cases of undue violence on the part of the police, in clashes between them. That violence on both sides came from mutual fear. The new foreigner generally feared some superior dexterity on the part of the Japanese, who in turn feared the superior size and the supposed superior strength of the foreigner. Each in consequence was likely to put forth in a quarrel greater violence than the occasion required, and no one on earth resents a blow with the hand more quickly and more fiercely than the Japanese. The Japanese does not fight except to disable or kill. Fighting is part of war. In older European days a blow with the hand was a blood insult to any gentleman, when the gentleman was a man of the sword. Perhaps part of the secret of this permanent misunderstanding lay in the fact that the Japanese clansman, like the Scot, was a gentleman no matter what lowly avocation he might pursue, and that the clansmen still gave the tone to Japanese society.

Business disagreements were common and led to much ill feeling. Japanese life was only slowly emerging from that of the great feudal clans of thirty years before. Not long since the money changer and the trader had moved on a lower plane, exactly as in the forgotten days of feudal Europe. The man of the sword was the gentleman. His point of honour was not expected in the money man. Consequently, American and European traders, tea and silk brokers, merchants, bankers, and business men generally, found in their dealings with native business points of comparison with the commercial Chinese which were all to the disadvantage of Japan. In some cases, such as the delivery of inferior goods or breaches of contract, it seemed that as often as not there was misunderstanding as to quality and nature of the goods or even as to the nature of a contract. In cases where intentional dishonesty was plain to be seen, it seemed that there might be reaction also to dubious or out-and-out dishonest methods of that lower foreign element which always follows legitimate business to far places.

Such tentative views were not popular, however, among the foreign business men or even among diplomats, and new-comers soon learned not to express them indiscriminately. We 'griffins' (tenderfeet) looked upon our chiefs of legation with considerable awe, and believed that to have obtained so exalted a position a man must know exactly what he was doing and why. That is not a belief that one retains long in diplomacy. There is such a thing as sitting through one's career. I doubt very much to-day that anyone had or could have a very clear picture in his mind of what it was all about. It is clear to-day that Japanese diplomacy, expansion and colonial policies could not possibly have been other than they were. There was not really any mystery about them at all.

Europe was a new and fearful phenomenon to the Japanese. They had decided, with a practical turn of mind reminiscent of Rome, that their people must become a nation, and their nation must be put on a footing of equality with European nations or perish. They were turning to their own practical uses everything they could learn about our Western ways, and using every particle of political and religious and dynastic force they possessed to mould their whole economy to that end. There were maladjustments of course. There was awkwardness; the tools were still new to their hand. There was swift suspicion, and a certain ruthlessness about them, a determination to win over all obstacles, that could inspire fear and distrust. There was a certain mysterious reserve, too, which baffled the callow penetration of the new-comers. We wondered what were the real thoughts and intentions behind the mask of such men as Matsukata, Hirobumi Ito, Okuma with the wooden leg, Saigo (with his European air), Nabeshima or the Tokugawa themselves to whom the new order of things meant as much as to the emperor. One went to their houses, and, in a way, one knew them. It was impossible not to respect these men, all of them great statesmen and some of them great gentlemen.

One should have understood. Their diplomacy was still that of the man of the sword and tempered by his code. They had not yet bred the civil servant. Nor had they bred that bourgeois middle class which gave to European diplomacy its tone of business backed by force.

I had come to Japan not only to study Japan, but to see European diplomacy in the making.

I had to go still farther East to see Japanese diplomacy in the making and its effect on Europe.

McKinley swept us all out of office. William Woodville Rockhill, one of the best rounded diplomats we have ever had (himself swept into the discard) insisted that I return to the East, where vital things were about to happen.

'Korea is the place,' he said. 'Nobody wants it; it is too

insignificant – but it is there you will see diplomacy in the raw; diplomacy without gloves, perfume or phrases. Don't chuck the job because the Department has let you down. Get out to Korea and watch. We need somebody to know what it is all about, and we ought not to take all our information from the chief conspirators.'

Senator Lodge secured me an appointment from the President to the only vacant post left; one that nobody wanted; one so unimportant in the eyes of the new assistant secretary of state that he was about to make me minister there, before, in my innocence, I told him I only aspired to be secretary; and I went to Korea.

CHAPTER II

KOREA

CHEMULPO was an unattractive entrance to a great adventure. Sharp from the tide line rose barren hills, not very high, naked of tree and bush, all dead brown sand and black granite rock. There was no animation in the port, a roundish space at the mouth of the Han River, enclosed by islands. Native sailing craft lay on the mud where the tide had left them. A few small coasting steamers anchored farther out, waiting for the seventeen feet of flow the turning tide would bring.

All along the quay rows of stolid natives squatted, watching, immovable, all dressed alike in baggy quilted cotton trousers and long dingy white cotton coats to the heels; all with their feet in straw sandals or wooden pattens fastened over thick padded cotton boots; with long-stemmed pipe in mouth, crammed with a golden-yellow tobacco cone like the base of a thick cheroot, and with hands thrust deep into opposite sleeves for warmth. Each head was topped off by a jaunty top knot, close braided and turned, the size of a man's two fingers – a most convenient grip in a scuffle. They were biggish men, some rather heavily bearded, many with light brown, grey or blue eyes, with reddish hair and ruddy complexion. At first sight one might be inclined to think the fairish colouring to be evidence of mixed blood, but ethnologists were not of that opinion. In spite of considerable mixture of blood from Japan and China through the centuries, the Korean is probably quite distinct from either in original stock, some element of the great migrations of

pre-history sidetracked in the peninsula, and touched
only at long intervals by its continental neighbours or by
sea wanderers from the Pacific islands.

Chemulpo, however, was only the entrance. The
interior had real charm. The country is all hills, like
frozen white caps, with hardly a wide valley between. It is
all granite, bare along most of the coast and central part,
but with a peaceful, still beauty which saved it from
monotony and justified the old name for Korea: 'the land
of morning calm.'

The local explanation of the deforestation is typical of
Korean ways: the coasts were made as uninviting as possible to discourage strangers, and in the interior whole
forests were burned off centuries ago, and the hills kept
bare until the top soil had washed down, in order to discourage tigers.

Cultivation lay along the valley bottoms and was
abundant, fields and villages following the river roads of
packed granite gravel. Rice was the staple, as in Japan, but
of a finer quality, much prized throughout the East.
Japanese rice fields are flooded during the growing
season, like Malayan padi, but in Korea much of it is
grown dry and thrives well. Other grains abound also, in
small hill fields; barley, some rye and wheat, peas and
beans. Unlike Japan, Korea had fine cattle, big and beefy,
and plentiful. Bulls were used for ploughing and all heavy
burdens, the horses being even smaller than in Japan and
China, not bigger than Welsh ponies. Wicked little beasts
these ponies were, as vicious in their sudden attacks along
the road as the Japanese fighting stallions, and far more
dangerous than the slow and rather peaceful bulls.

Unlike Japan, too, pigs poked about the doors and
chickens were plentiful. Innumerable dogs, hordes of
masterless dogs, snapped at the heels of every traveller
and were the bane of the first missionaries who came (in
spite of exclusion laws) disguised as native mourners,
their foreign faces veiled. They might pass the natives

muffled and 'under vow of silence' but not the dogs. Even after decades of free intercourse a foreigner still threw all native animals into paroxysms of rage and fear.

Through the valleys, along and above the stony watercourses ran roads and paths, with clustering villages every few miles, shaded by superb chestnut or ginkei trees.

The houses were uniformly of one storey, with mud walls and heavy peaked thatched roofs, on which red peppers were spread to dry, brilliant in the sun – for the sun can shine in Korea, even in winter.

Tobacco hung drying along the eaves, with garlic and mushrooms, and everywhere near the villages pheasants crowed or chuckled at the field edges. Wild geese and ducks rooted in the paddy fields; giant bustards flocked in the open grass lands.

These cottage rooms are small and well heated by hot air passing under the floor from the furnace mouth at one end of the house on the outside, to the chimney at the other end. All cooking is done outside at the furnace mouth, with twigs, dried grass, old bean pods or any other rubbish as fuel. The interiors could be immaculately clean, but generally are infested with vermin, called, as in Japan, 'the China bug.' The floors are built of flat stones placed on edge to form channels running through the length of the house in a sort of maze. Over these other flat stones are laid, and on that a layer of mud, hardened and smoothed and covered with layers of thick oiled paper which takes with age a fine mahogany colour. Walls and windows are covered with thin but very strong white paper. This paper is of a superior quality; one very tough variety used for wrapping is made from a bush akin to poison oak, after the juice is extracted for lacquer.

Thin mattresses about two feet wide serve as seats and beds, upon the floor. Tall brass candlesticks light the low carved wooden tables used for reading, or upon which food is served. Meal time is any time the master wants his food. It is the women's business to see that he gets it promptly; it is abundant and varied, covered with red pepper and served in polished brass bowls with plentiful libations of a powerful brandy made of rice. Only warm rice water will relieve the devastating effect of the fiery red pepper with which all food is soaked.

Better houses are raised high from the ground on foundations of cut granite blocks, the walls framed in heavy chestnut, walnut or oaken pillars supporting the high tiled roof and sweeping graceful eaves. Fine straw mats cover the oiled-paper floors; painted screens and beautifully polished brass-bound hard-wood chests and presses furnish the rooms; Chinese paintings or some finely written classic or original poem ornament the walls.

Poetry is the language of all who aspire to a classic education. Poems are even chiselled upon the granite rocks at some waterfall, mountain pass or specially famous view, much more peaceful than our way of decorating the landscape with advertising posters. In the spring flood time parties of old gentlemen go out on fishing parties, angling, jigging or with cast nets. After the day's catch the evenings are spent in poetical contests and music, stimulated by abundant native wine.

City houses or country houses of great nobles have the service offices and quarters, stables and guard houses on the street or roadside, with one or many interior courts and gardens completely sheltered by high walls and beautifully laid out according to the rank, wealth, and taste of the owner.

Every Korean noble, in addition to his great house, keeps somewhere a tiny place, hidden away in the mountains but always in particularly beautiful surroundings, to which he disappears for solitude from time to time, or in which he withdraws from public life when politics are shaky. There seemed to be a rather rigid etiquette about these tiny refuges; except in case of high treason a man was rarely disturbed by enemies, never by friends when it was known that he had 'gone to the country.' Some patri-

archal families of great wealth never came to the capital–
and only the capital counted to the noble as 'town.' One
old gentleman of a southern province had parcelled his
rice lands out among some four hundred hereditary
tenant families. Every day of the year each one of these
families owed him in turn twenty-four hours' service in
the house, bringing all food consumed there during their
service, for themselves and the master's family. The
village paid all the taxes, for themselves and him, and
supplied him annually with cotton and native silk goods
sufficient for his family equipment in clothes. On these
conditions they used their land free and had done so for
immemorial generations. The burden fell lightly on all
concerned and since it was his land and his village there
was no law and no government. Everything ran quietly by
custom. In rare cases of dispute or difficulty the master's
'advice' was sought and taken.

Slavery existed in Korea, but only feminine slavery. In
the lowest servant class, girl children were born unfree,
and could never leave the master's service without his
consent. It was a gentle slavery, not onerous in most
cases. When the slave girl came to marriageable age, she
settled down in the house or on the estate with some
young free man as husband, to whom a liberal ration of
rice and other food and clothes was made in lieu of payment for his sevices to the master. Of their children the
boys were free, the daughters unfree.

Religion in Korea was a curious affair. People believed
in one God, all good and kindly, but very remote from the
simple everyday business of mankind. Devils, on the
contrary, swarmed like disease germs and microbes
everywhere, and it was very necessary to placate and
deceive them. Rather stupid devils they were, in a way, for
they could be deceived; their power for evil was unlimited,
but their power to see a man's thoughts did not go farther
than that of an intelligent man. What devils wanted was
worship. One might pretend to worship them with

elaborate ritual, and so placate them and prevent mis-
chief, and God who does know men's hearts and minds,
would not hold it against men doing their poor best.
Every great tree in a village and every mountain pass had
its malign or tutelary spirit. Sacrifice was made to devils
by giving some part of one's self– spitting was enough, or
a rag torn from one's clothes and hung on a bush; or a
stone piled on an ever-growing heap nearby, or for blood,
a handful of sprinkled chicken feathers. This belief was
thoroughly abused, even in high places, by professional
devil priests and sorceresses, whose incantations, heavily
paid, were necessary in illness. Among the upper classes,
men were impatient of these practices but the women
held to them, and men in the Orient have discovered in
some thousands of years that it is best to be at peace with
the women-folk, even at some slight sacrifice – not
necessarily a part of this same general devil worship. Men
had their own beliefs and held to the diviner or fortune
teller, whose importance lay in the selection of a pro-
pitious grave site through which succeeding generations
would be prosperous. That had the advantage of being
connected with astrology and of being thereby scientific
and more dignified than devil worship.

Women ruled the household, in spite of their rigid
seclusion. In Japan women had a society of their own, and
even in public places men might greet and speak to them,
provided the conversation were guarded by formal
ceremony. In the early centuries of the Christian era, the
society of Japanese court lords and ladies showed some
resemblance to the troubadour society of southern
France. Women in Korea, however, were strictly guarded,
so strictly that it was considered safer to hide and shield
an intruder than to denounce him. The better class went
veiled when outside of their own inner quarters of the
house. They were a power in the house, nevertheless. A
man might have only one wife, though he might have as
many private establishments outside as his means permit-

ted. Boys born outside the house might be presented to a family council of elders at a certain age, and received into the family or not as these decreed.

Family life was based upon some ancient clan system. There were comparatively few family names, like Ye (the royal clan), Min (the oldest and most noble of the clans), and Pak. To these clan names, which always came first, was added a generation name, common to all brothers and first cousins, and finally a personal name. Thus Min Yong Whan, Min Yong Ik, Min Yong In, etc., would be immediately known as persons of the same generation of the Min family, brothers or first cousins. There were hereditary court families always sure of high office, but minor officials might be drawn from any class into the nine categories of official life, appointment to office constituting nobility.

Out in the thickly forested Diamond Mountains and in sheltered wooded places up and down the land were Buddhist monasteries of monks and nuns. In one of the three old kingdoms out of which Korea grew, Buddhism had once held high rank. Nobles and even royal persons entered these monasteries, as in feudal Europe. At the time of the great Japanese invasion, in the sixteenth century, from which Korea has never recovered, precious stores of ancient writings were looted and taken back to Japan (together with the casks of pickled ears of slaughtered Koreans, the origin of the famous 'mound of ears' in the old Japanese capital). Before that, Buddhism had become tainted with worldly ambition, and after an unsuccessful attempt to seize all power, the monks were decimated and banished from the cities. They fell on evil days as time went on, and lived by begging, recruiting their novices from waifs and orphaned beggar children. As a class, they were illiterate and superstitious, but exceedingly kindly and hospitable. Their temples, always placed in picturesque and peaceful spots, were charming resting places, whether one might be travelling or shooting. Big game was plentiful in the mountain forests in which the temples lay – tigers, leopards, bears, wolves, wild boars of great size and fierceness, and deer.

Koreans gave the impression of a nomadic people recently settled in villages and towns. There were ruins of cities and palaces of considerable size and evident wealth, and in lonely places cromlechs and dolmens like those of Brittany and western England. Their attitude toward the outside world, its ways and its inventions was what might have been the bewilderment of the Israelites of Abraham's time, confronted with railways, trolley cars and the intricacies of European politics. They did not understand any of it and did not want it. They wanted to be let alone in their 'Hermit Kingdom.'

Their history goes back into the twilight. Affected very early by Chinese culture, their civilization stood at one time higher than that of Japan. Early Japan raided habitually along the coast and twice invaded in force. The second time, in the sixteenth century, there was a special cause for the dispatch of a great army of conquest. Japan was in danger of becoming Catholic. Korea, according to tradition which it would be interesting to investigate, offered a solution to the Tycoon. He despatched a Christian army of conquest, so the story goes, and hard on its heels another, a 'pagan army' under old Kato of Choshiu, so that, caught between it and the enemy, the first might not return. Down from the North flowed a vast horde from China to meet them, the Christian army was crushed; Korea was swept bare – her cities devastated, her monastic libraries sacked and destroyed, her potters and porcelain-makers transported bodily to Japan to develop what has become known as a characteristic Japanese art, the Satsuma ware. Perhaps these captive Koreans became the pariah class of Japan, the Eta, whose origins are unknown.

There is another tradition of this time, accepted by Koreans as historic. It is recorded in the imperial family archives that the invasion was broken by the ingenuity of a Korean general or 'admiral' who covered a great wooden junk with heavy iron plates, attached an iron ram to her prow and broke the Japanese communications with his one vessel. There seems to have been no *Monitor* to his *Merrimac* – or rather to his *Tennessee*, for the description corresponds more nearly with the latter.

Japan and China each claimed suzerainty over the prostrate country, each receiving unwilling tribute until the Chinese-Japanese war in 1894 when China was decisively defeated and renounced all claims. Korea, however, slipped a delegation through the Japanese fleet to Washington, at the suggestion of resident Americans, and brought back recognition as a treaty-making power, therefore, sovereign and independent.

Seoul is the heart of the nation and the centre of its life much more than Peking or Tokyo is the centre of Chinese or Japanese national life. Seoul is to Korea much more than Paris is to France, for the older cities have decayed and fallen into ruined palaces and avenues surrounded by clusters of semi-isolated villages within ancient city walls. Only Peng Yang, in the north, had a distinct and native life of its own, and was known as one of the four wickedest cities of ancient and modern times.

Up to the capital from the River Han, flowing swift and green through a wide gravel bed left from yearly spring floods, broad roads led through populous villages, pine-clad knolls and hillside cemeteries to the city lying in a broad valley protected on all sides by spurs running down from the stark peaks of Puk Han Mountain, the city walls and towers following the ridge. From the leisurely ferries an ever-increasing stream of white-clad figures, pony and bullock trains moved slowly up, through the tower gates, at which traitors' heads were still exposed, and into the two great intersecting avenues, the city's main arteries, the work of Sir John McLeavy Brown. The city walls, of well-joined granite, wide enough at the top to make a comfortable walk, wander over the tops of the hills, topped with pine, and in season aflame with azaleas of all hues, rhododendron and plum blossoms, and join a higher line of defence crowning the massive rock citadel of the Puk Han Range, a place of temples and monasteries, and a refuge by narrow and precipitous paths for bygone kings in time of public danger.

The city was divided into wards, each with its name, in older days the grouping place of clans, nobles' houses or guilds. In the northern wards lay the great abandoned palaces, the new palace of the emperor's father, the dynamic regent – the eastern palace where the progressive little queen was murdered, and the old western palace, sometimes the haunt of a stray wolf or leopard, all their majestic halls and lovely parks decaying. Several broad sewer canals ran through the city, bridged by fine, polished marble arches; narrow foetid lanes circled through the wards, and lesser, deep, stone-lined canals with entrance bridges of logs or boards to doorways on either side – an unnavigable Venice. House refuse lay scattered and heaped in these canals and lanes; except in mountain flood time a trickle of green scummy water oozed along the bottom, carrying typhoid, smallpox, and cholera. In these pools women cheerfully washed their clothes and prepared their daily food, no worse place than the shallow wells reeking with surface drainage. In the squalid lower quarters, smelling to the skies of *Kim-Chee*, the national condiment, made of cabbage and turnips well rotted together, hordes of dogs snapped and yelled, like the famous masterless dogs of Constantinople. Sometimes one happened on the work of the dog-butcher, lassoing some stray cur, swinging him choking and snarling till he died and boiling the foul and sickly smelling meat for the consumption of those who could not buy good beef. Here, as in Israel, dogs and pigs are scavengers, and one realizes suddenly why, in the Mosaic law, they were unclean.

Around the intersection of the two great main streets clustered the better shops: chickens, pheasants, eggs and black unbled beef were offered for sale. There was an abundance of vegetables manured from the city sewers, in addition to the national food staple, a fine quality of rice. Silks, native and Chinese brocades, cotton piece goods, green and red slippers for women, black and white slippers for men, straw sandals for workers or travellers, sandals woven of white paper string for mourners were displayed in Turkish-looking booths. Iron tobacco boxes inlaid with threads of nickel or silver, brass, nickel or silver pipe bowls and bundles of reed stems, yard long for the nobles, twelve inches in length for the commoner, and cones of sun-cured, aromatic yellow pipe tobacco lay out on trays before the shallow shops.

In the very centre, under a curving roof, lay 'the voice of the city,' the great bell of Chong No, one of the largest in the world, to the making of which women brought their gold and silver, and one her child, cast into the fused metal as a propitiatory sacrifice. Its deep booming roar could be heard in every part of town and out in the far mountains, with its wailing overtone, the voice of the sacrificed child. In and around this centre drifted stately, idle, white figures, thousands of men, unobservant of the crowd, disinterested till some sudden happening crystallized them into an excited mob; women of the lower respectable classes trotted through the crowd, their faces veiled, but for one black curious eye, by a green mantle covering the head, unconscious of the wide gap between the tops of their baggy trousers and the narrow-sleeved jacket covering their arms and the tops of their shoulders. Ladies borne in closed sedan chairs by two running coolies, invisible but keenly observant through the bamboo screens of their boxlike conveyance, glided through the throng. Boys with long pigtails and little unveiled girls in pink dodged in and out, flying paper dragon kites, spinning tops, playing hop-scotch or battledore and shuttlecock with their feet, or crying hot chestnuts for sale. Squads of soldiers, armed with antiquated single-shot rifles, Berdan or Gras, the cullings of the European armies of 1870, moved slowly from post to post. For greater safety they carried no ammunition, but the long slender lancelike bayonet remained eternally fixed. Officers scurried past on shambling China ponies. Here and there a gentleman on horseback, perched high on a native saddle and robed in starched immaculate white, with flowing over-robe of lively coloured silk gauze, was led through the streets by a running groom, or some great noble passed with his retinue, grave and solemn, his open fan before his face, borne high in his massive carrying chair on the shoulders of four men, four relay carriers running behind, an attendant valet at each side bearing pipe and seal and portfolio, an obsequious secretary panting to keep up, a little cloud of policemen, sabres clanking, and of runners armed with staves opening a way for His Excellency's progress through the trains of biting, squealing pack ponies and obstinate, heavily laden bulls.

Over the house walls droop innumerable flowering shrubs and much Forsythia, here called apropriately 'canari'; over all, in the crystal-clear sky wheel flocks of parti-coloured magpies, and kites calling like the far-off whinny of an Arab horse. From the hills come singing, long-drawn quavering notes, melancholy with mountain sadness, or lilting cheerily in the clear air, and from the houses, at night, the throbbing of the hour-glass drum, tapped at one end with a flexible bamboo slip, rubbed lightly with the fingers at the other; the droning of native bagpipes and the wail of reed flutes mingle with the eternal tapping of women's ironing sticks as they smooth their lords' garments to shining whiteness for the next day's wear abroad.

Night is the women's time; then they wash, iron, prepare the morrow's food, visit, gossip or quarrel shrilly for all the world to know. Men sleep at night, visit, or go to court. By ancient custom all the palace wakes at night, for safety's sake.

CHAPTER III

THE DIPLOMATIC CORPS AND THE FOREIGN COLONIES AT SEOUL

IT is the fashion nowadays for professors and publicists to write and lecture of imperialism as a major evil of diplomacy. There is no doubt that with a correct definition it is so. The trouble, as always, lies in the definition. Most people are writing about it only from hearsay. There is a great difference between seeing a thing and writing about it from hearsay, and I think one needs to have lived in the atmosphere out of which this imperialism grew and to have played one's part in it, however small and unimportant, to understand exactly what professors are trying to say.

In retrospect Seoul offers the most perfect example I have ever seen of the 'machinery of imperialism' in the front line, which they describe to-day in theory.

The southern wards of Seoul, all that part lying toward the river gates, were occupied by the legations and the foreign colonies. The position was strategic in the military sense, of course, and it was quite intentionally so, for when the city was first opened to foreign residence one chose the site best suited to swift and easy retreat in case of sudden outbreak of hostility. That was true of most cities in the Far East where foreigners lived. It was often necessary to withdraw. In Japan the foreign legations were withdrawn at one time to Yokohama, where they could be more easily defended; the Japanese legation and colony were withdrawn several times from Korea and in earlier days our own minister to Korea was permitted to live as far off as Chefoo, in China, though the naval attaché, Foulke, remained at the legation in Seoul and saved the situation.

In this southern district of the city nearly all the foreigners lived; each group was headed by its legation or consulate, and each group contained its church interests, its commercial body, its nationals employed in the native government, all focusing on the palace, all outwardly cordial to each other, but in reality all highly competitive and suspicious. Into the western section of this legation quarter where Europeans and Americans congregated, the emperor had slipped for refuge after the murder of his queen, and occupied a new, crude, hasty structure lacking all dignity and grace, built on vacant land adjoining the American legation and British consulate general, dominated by and connected with the Russian legation. Its only important feature was the huge granite wall that surrounded and protected it.

Over opposite the Russians lay the French legation, furnished with beautiful old things sent out from one of the historic châteaux of the Loire. Opposite the Americans lay the German consulate, and in the centre at each end of the narrow walled legation street stood the American missionaries' club and tennis courts, and the shabby little diplomatic club.

Around each of these legations grouped houses of their nationals, schools, hospitals, and mission establishments. Farther east began the Chinese quarter, built around the old resident's yamen so long the official seat of the famous Yuan Shi Kai, who was later president of China, and might have been emperor. The yamen was then still occupied byTang Shao Yi, that able and cultured gentleman, a graduate of Yale, whose logical position during the Boxer disorders was so tragically misunderstood by both sides, since he was both patriotically Chinese and clearly convinced that some, but not all, Western ways and things were good for China.

Beyond, from the south to near the east gate, was the

Japanese town, at the foot of the green South Mountain, overlooked by the Japanese legation and barracks, shaded by age-old fern trees. The Japanese minister, even when he was not the dean of the diplomatic body, generally took on the air of a resident, above and apart from the general ruck of diplomatic representatives (and each consul here had diplomatic functions). Other legations had marine guards, from a sergeant's squad to a company. He had a miniature army, with artillery, cavalry and infantry, engineers and field telegraph corps. A considerable body of army officers of rank was attached to him, moving through the country, sometimes openly and in uniform, sometimes as private travellers *en civile*, sometimes even disguised. Up in the northern country once, I met a poor Japanese pedlar, whose face attracted me, for it indicated breeding above his apparent condition. I asked him for information as to roads in the Tumen district, over against Vladivostok and Russian territory. He was dull and ignorant and, of course, knew no foreign language, and understood my Japanese with greatest difficulty, if at all. Months later I had a letter in excellent French from a major of the general staff in Tokyo, who appeared to know very well who I was, apologizing for the incident and for his 'discourtesy' since he was on special mission when I met him, and telling me how I could get a good map of the northern provinces of Korea, published in Japan by the general staff.

The Japanese minister lived in his citadel as in a feudal castle, his neat and bustling private town at his feet; his army at his command; his police and gendarmes' barracks, his consulate, his consular court, his police courts, his schools and newspaper offices about him; and to be complete, his group of Buddhist priests, brought over to study the remaining vestiges of Buddhism in Korea. In spite of much assurance that the legation could exercise no control whatever over Japanese subjects in the town, the Japanese quarter was, in fact, a Japanese city within the capital, in which the minister could use all but absolute power over his people, whether he possessed it legally or not.

The Chinese resident had exercised the function of a moderator in the affairs of the Korean king. The Japanese minister grew to act habitually as if he had succeeded to that office, or rather, as if he had expelled from it a usurper.

Over against him for power and influence stood Horace N. Allen, our minister and consul general, another example of the fact that our haphazard methods of appointment were often luckier than they deserved to be. More than average tall, extremely thin, lanky even, as Lincoln was lanky, as bald as it is possible to be, with a jutting Wellingtonian nose and peaked, flaming-red, aggressive beard, he looked as unlike the usual formal diplomat as may be, but no one could mistake him for anything but a man of strong character, softened by a tender heart and wise in the ways of Koreans. Moreover, Allen was distinctly an American. Once when his predecessor, a clergyman as well as American minister, was holding service in the English chapel at the time of Cleveland's Venezuela ultimatum, and had just offered a prayer for the confusion of the queen's enemies, Allen was heard to remark, regardless of the place, that he did not think that prayer an appropriate one at that moment, to which every Englishman present agreed.

There was not a diplomat of them all who possessed the confidence of emperor and people as Allen did. Others might cajole or bully; it was to Allen that the emperor turned for advice or consolation. He had come out from Ohio as a medical missionary, an excellent physician. In one of the palace uprisings the powerful chief of the queen's clan, the great Prince Min, had been left for dead. Dr Allen cared for him, sheltered him and cured him, and secured in the normal course of his profession an influence based on solid gratitude and trust which was to serve him well as a diplomat. When after the Japan-China war, Korea smuggled a mission through to Washington, Allen was asked to go along and guide them. Returning successful, he had been appointed secretary of legation, and now with the McKinley administration he was minister.

He presided over a considerable body of American interest. The Seoul-Chemulpo railway, the first to be developed, had made rapid progress in the hands of Americans; the most prosperous gold mine, the first power house, electric light plant, public telephone system and water works, all first-rate work, were built and operated or owned by Americans. A trolley line, built at the emperor's request from the palace to the queen's tomb outside the city, as a sort of luxurious toy, had extended to be a real public utility.

Tied in with these was a powerful church interest. Methodists, North and South, Presbyterians and others had their hospitals, orphanages, schools and mission stations and very active medical centres not only here in the capital but all through the bigger cities. Both in their schools and in their family lives the natives came into familiar contact with American thought and practice.

Next to the business and church interest in the American colony came the group of American advisers to the government. In the imperial household was Gen. Charles Legendre, a French volunteer, who was breveted brigadier-general in our Civil War for gallantry in action, of which he bore the scars. He was sent to Japan by President Grant to aid in reconstructing the government and after distinguished service there and in Formosa he had passed over to the Korean government with the full approval of the Japanese because of his former connection with them; of the French because of his birth; and of the Americans because of his Civil War record. General Dye, another Civil War veteran, had been loaned by

Grant to the Khedive of Egypt, and was now at the head of the Korean military school, which was turning out such good material that they had Korean cadets going from Dye to the Imperial Academy at Tokyo, and graduating there half a dozen together at the very top of their classes. 'General' G. had once been consul *general* at a treaty port in Japan, hence his military title. He had been a political power in a southern State and editor at one time of a leading western newspaper. He was a first-rate lawyer, rarely sober, but a remarkable man. The drunker he got the more lucid he became. Nothing he drank ever muddled his brain, though it might paralyse his body. On one occasion I had an intricate legal tangle to solve, and sent to him for advice. 'General' G. sat down with a bottle of Scotch whisky to sober up on which he sipped with half plain water and a lump of sugar to each tumbler. When he had finished that and another half-bottle, sitting on the floor after the first, he recapitulated his argument and asked: 'Have you got it now? Is it clear? Speak quickly, I am going off,' and as soon as I had proved that I had it, G. collapsed unconscious and was carried home by his servants.

Clarence Greathouse of Kentucky was law adviser to the Koreans and accomplished much in forming a legal procedure and establishing a principle in the native law and its application. For solid and permanent achievement he should rank with Sir John McLeavy Brown.

Finally there was 'Colonel' Ninstead. No one knew what his functions were in the Korean government, though he wore their military uniform. Probably he did not either. He had been a pay clerk in the American navy and perhaps fancied himself paymaster-general of the unpaid imperial forces. At regular intervals he promoted himself by having a new uniform made with the insignia of a higher rank.

The American tradition in Korea was an old one. In the 'eighties an American, Judge W. N. Denny, was drawn to the service of the Korean government and was given actual executive powers. He was not only an adviser. He was head of a department and a member of the government in as far as any minister of state could be said to be that. For a time it seemed as if he would be able to initiate the Koreans into the mysteries of responsible government, and no doubt he started with high hopes as did his successors, but the fragments of his correspondence which turned up once in a while showed gradual disheartenment with the impossibility of teaching an unwilling oriental people the basis of such a constitutional system as the American upon which his own ideas were based, and showed also the gradual hardening of a more definite Japanese policy toward Korea. Vestiges of his work remained, in spite of the inertia of the Koreans themselves. On what had been his experimental farm, a herd of wild, unbroken horses ran over what had been grain fields, while other fields were rented out for the private benefit of the native director who still drew a salary twenty-five years later, though the farm had long since ceased to exist.

No story of Korea, or of Japan either, is complete without Foulke. Attached to the Asiatic squadron immediately upon his graduation from the naval academy he found in his commanding officer an ardent student of Japanese art. Foulke quickly perfected himself in those studies and in the language. There is a tradition in our older navy of his romance. At Nagasaki in those days there was a quiet tea house in the hills kept by an old man and his wife with a lovely daughter who, to the surprise of American midshipmen, spoke English well and fluently. It was an orderly house, almost austere, and it was noticed that the old couple treated their daughter with great deference, and would allow no foreigner who was not everything that an officer and gentleman should be to enter, much less speak to the girl. It became a sort of club for a certain group of young middies, who delighted in the conversation of the daughter. She and Foulke, however, spoke only Japanese together, and soon to the exclusion of the rest. He married her, and the story has it that in the great war between the Satsuma and Choshiu clans, a very noble Choshiu family had been wiped out, all but a baby girl, who was rescued and carried away by two of the upper servants. They moved to the port and supported themselves and her by keeping this exclusive tea house for people who would not be likely to recognize her. Foulke was later sent to Korea as naval attaché and remained there when the legation was withdrawn to Chefoo for safety. He became an expert in Korean as he was in Japanese things. Much of American prestige in Korea and the confidence given to Americans was due to him. He carried the legation out of his own salary; no expenses were ever repaid him, for the legation had been withdrawn. Eventually he resigned from the navy, settled in Japan and became a Japanese; years later he was picked up dead one day on the road to Nikko. Some day when his story is pieced together it will make good reading.

These two groups of national interest, Japanese and American, represent fairly well the general type of what has since come to be called the machinery of imperialistic diplomacy.

The Belgian legation existed only as a screen for Russian intrigue. The Italians occasionally detached some charming, capable, and disinterested naval officer, like poor Francesetti, who died there of typhoid, for special duty as temporary consul. The Germans, Weipert, a gentle scholarly orientalist and mystic, and Krien, a jovial cynic, seemed to have no definite policy and fished for the Fatherland in muddy and troubled waters. M. Collin de Plancy for France was serious, courtly and discreet, allied with the Russians but aloof from all intrigue.

Mr John Jordan, now Sir John, headed a group similar to the Americans and controlled a real power through McLeavy Brown.

When Sir Robert Hart formed his first-rate Chinese customs service, Korea was included as part of it. When Korea's affairs were separated from China, the local Commissioner of Customs McLeavy Brown, with his international staff became the only solid and really efficient body of officials the Korean government possessed. Since the commissioner was an Englishman, protection of the Koren customs service in Korea was assumed by the British government, and when the Russian minister attempted to displace him in favour of M. Alexeieff, nine British cruisers gathered quietly in Chemulpo harbour and McLeavy Brown shipped all the customs funds to Shanghai on deposit, to be held there until the question should be decided.

In order to keep the customs revenues from being wasted by greedy native officials, and to preserve intact a fund which was the only one, and therefore had to serve for public improvements or as a basis for a possible foreign loan for constructive purposes, McLeavy Brown was forced to be arbitrary about its management. It is all very well now to write theoretically about the illegal acts of foreigners engaged in trying to build solid foundations of government in such countries as Korea. The thing cannot even be discused intelligently without considering that there was no law but the will of an absolute monarch, who was a pleasant, good-natured man with no will power at all and no understanding of anything that was happening in the world about him. I think that it is not the activities of devoted and intelligent public servants like McLeavy Brown which call for criticism, but, if a general world condition can be criticized, the fact that national jealousy and trivial competition among the Western powers was a complete bar to anybody's attempt to remould an ancient civilization to its modern needs.

The real trouble was that with the first-rate men they had in Korea the English could not co-operate with us to pull things together because of the higher diplomacy which subordinated everything to the Japanese alliance.

Another Englishman who did most excellent service for Korea was Hutchison, the head of the English school for Korean boys. He ran it as an English public school, and curiously enough his Korean boys responded splendidly to his system. I recall one who went straight from him to the School of Mines in London, graduated with honours and returned to an important position in a foreign mining company in Korea. Hutchison's school, like all the other foreign-language schools, was subsidized by the Korean government.

The widow of a British consul had been made governess of the infant prince and, as such, held some vague oriental rank, but had no functions beyond receiving her precarious pay.

The Church of England was represented by Bishop Corfe, a former chaplain of the fleet, by his saintly successor, Arthur Turner, a famous athlete, and by the present Bishop Mark Trollope, three as priestly men as one would be likely to see.

As in Tokyo, the Russian representation moved from simple kindly bureaucrats to cyclonic individuals who brought their country to the verge of war, and the Russian legation was always an uncertain and disturbing factor.

Besides their groups of vague concession hunters, solid business men, nationals on the Korean government payroll with more or less defined functions, and the various church interests, each legation chief and diplomatic consul also maintained an organized native group within the palace. Each had an official native interpreter for whom he demanded access to the palace at any time. Each interpreter was the go-between for his chief with someone in the palace, from the chief eunuch down to the personal servants of the emperor.

The court was full of idle, hungry native place hunters who watched the influence of each legation with hawk-eyes and paid court accordingly.

In addition, it was customary to form a party around some high official connected with the legations either by conviction or by his purse strings.

The higher eunuchs alone had access to majesty at all hours, as guardians and attendants of the Sacred Person. They were the emperor's news-gatherers and retailed the gossip of the day during his toilet and idle hours. Flattery, presents, money bribes flowed to these people in a thousand different ways to create a favourable atmosphere.

In a country unfamiliar with Western ways everyone in the corps had usurped a privilege theoretically accorded only to ambassadors. They claimed the right to see the emperor at will and to oblige him to discuss any and all matters pertaining to their interests. Of course this was an outcome of the absolute power of the emperor and the impotence of his state ministers, though many of these were earnest, patriotic and, within their limits, competent men. It was an abuse, nevertheless. Every consul and diplomat felt that audience must be demanded at frequent intervals, even if he had to drag out a simple inquiry about the emperor's health over a full hour if possible, in mysterious whispers. This seemed to enhance national prestige in some such way as cheering by stopwatch, at national conventions, indicates the popularity of a Republican or Democratic candidate for the presidency.

Every time a foreign representative was given such an audience his colleagues devoted the rest of the week to finding out, through whatever secret channels they possessed, just what he had said.

Every one of the legations and consulates got what it could according to its strength except the Italians. I do not count the Chinese, for they asked nothing after their great defeat by the Japanese and the final retirement from Korea of Tang Shao Yi. From that time on their personal protection was assumed by the British government and they went about their lawful avocations without politics.

Things were done without warrant in the international code of diplomatic usage, not only to the helpless Koreans but among members of the diplomatic corps to each other. Everything turned upon concessions, that is, upon obtaining by intimidation, cajolery or bribery, licence to exploit for foreign interest some source of revenue of the Korean government. Whenever a legation succeeded in wresting a concession from the emperor, every colleague demanded a similar one, on the basis of some 'favoured nation' clause of his commercial treaty with Korea, which of course had nothing to do with the matter.

Korea is the best illustration of this transition period of diplomacy, because it was the weakest of the Far Eastern countries, not only weak internally but also by having no undisputed official protector or friend among the Western powers. In China the same sort of thing was going on, but China is practically a continent, and the ancient power of China still lingered in European race memories as the seat of the King of Kings and the source of the invasions across the Russian steppes which almost swallowed Europe. China was still a power, while Korea is a relatively small country; all its public life centred in the capital and the very thoughts of its rulers lay open to any-one's study. Whatever may have been the policy of Japan and the British government, however, in keeping national policies clearly before their representatives' eyes, the State Department confined itself to general abstractions. In so remote a spot we only guessed at home policy by the daily papers which arrived six weeks to two months late, and guided our activities by what the editors might think European nations seemed to be doing to each other.

Our nearest guess about England, for example, would be that suspicion of Russia's probable intentions in India had simply been transferred to the Pacific, and since nobody knew anything of the terms of the new alliance with Japan any more than anybody knew what the Triple Alliance covered, that mysterious new document hung over us like a menace of war. Only one thing seemed certain about it, that whatever Japan might do in Korea would be supported by the British consul general.

The same secret relation seemed to exist between Russia and France, except that the French minister held himself aloof from all personal intrigue. Nobody knew how strong the Russian autocracy might be. Its power was taken for granted. Nobody at that time could suspect that it was as weak as it turned out to be.

Russia was penetrating everywhere upon the eastern and northern Asiatic continent and seemed in a fair way to become the greatest of Asiatic powers as well as a power in Europe. Whatever Russia's dark intentions might be it seemed fairly certain that ice-free ports in the Pacific must be part of their preparation. Korea was in direct line in that advance, and Korea's land's end was quite too close to the very heart of Japan, only a few hours' full steam. That much was perfectly clear of what Japan's situation must be. Nobody believed that Japan could stand alone against the enormous weight of Russia. Many wondered to what extent the British fleet could balance the Russian colossus plus France. The atmosphere of the East in the late 'nineties was of war.

In the meantime, Russia's fleet wintered habitually in Japan's southern island, in the harbour of Nagasaki, and those of us who knew Japan knew also that this custom was an unfortunate one for Russia.

Little by little astute Japanese observers must become aware of weak spots where strength was essential. In their habitual cynical indifference to public opinion Russian naval officers and the commissariat made no attempt to conceal their enormous peculations. In official graft there was nothing to choose between most of the fleet commanders and Chinese or Korean officials, the one notorious exception being Admiral Dubassoff. All supply or construction and repair accounts were padded to sums made possible only by connivance of the ministry of marine and the treasury at St Petersburg, and everybody knew it. The same system of graft was perfectly well known in all the shipyards where Russian cruisers were built abroad.

It was in the harbour of Nagasaki that Russia lost the war of 1904; it was there that the Japanese learned that no matter how fine and gallant the Russian might be personally, no efficient fighting machine that is based upon official corruption can endure long.

CHAPTER IV

THE EMPEROR

THE centre of all intrigue that was the life of Seoul was the king, recently become emperor and, theoretically, monarch of all he surveyed. According to Korean theory both the land was his, and the people. After the Chinese model, he had his ministers of state of course, but they were his servants, meant to carry out his will and to act as buffers between him and the foreign diplomats, who persistently confused these figureheads with responsible cabinet ministers, till, finding that they had no responsibility and could make no decisions that might not be reversed in His Majesty's next conversation with the parties concerned, they grew into the way of taking everything, even the most trivial matters, straight to the palace. It came to be a sure sign of loss of favour and influence to be referred back to a ministry of state from the palace, and the really serious defect in the system was that the emperor had no will.

Soon after my arrival I was presented at court by Doctor Allen. Although the palace side gate opened not twenty yards from the legation entrance, it was not good form for a high dignitary to enter on foot. We were carried in sedan chairs covered with green cloth, with four carriers each and a tail of private guards or Kisu in ancient soldiers' garb, who at other times were gate keepers, messengers and men of all work, but when in uniform claimed a certain mild deference from the populace as belonging to the retinue of some powerful noble.

Warning shouts of our approach began before we left

the legation compound, relayed by watchers to the palace gate across the street and in to the inner courts, and at a running walk our chairs deposited us at the door of a shabby little brick cottage, very different from the great hall of the ambassadors in the old palaces.

In this place, scantily furnished with cheap and gaudy carpets and Grand Rapids mission chairs, the minister of the household, the minister for foreign affairs and the master of ceremonies received us, with several court interpreters and several gentlemen known to be friendly to Americans. The emperor's uncle joined the party, a shrewd and merry gentleman of great bulk known among foreigners by his nickname the 'fat prince,' but not so well known for the remarkable astuteness concealed under his gay temper and lazy manners. Then followed a eunuch of high rank to warn us of the emperor's approach to the audience hall, and a palace servant in magenta robes and hairy felt hat with peacocks' plumes, to lead the way. The two ministers of state went first, mounted the granite steps and prostrated themselves, fully, three times, advancing each time until they rose from the last obeisance before the emperor and a little to each side, where they stood with bent heads and downcast eyes, arms crossed on the breast. The interpreter followed with the same ceremony, and Doctor Allen and I, with three bows instead of genuflections arrived in front of a small table behind which stood His Majesty and his oldest son the crown prince, backed by a gorgeous, golden-painted screen – concealing some living thing, for there was much soft rustling, whispering and once a tiny giggle, sternly repressed by eunuchs.

The audience was very brief. The emperor, a white-faced little man, eager and timid in manner, was clothed in marvellous golden silk embroidered with the imperial dragon. He greeted us warmly, friendly and without ceremony. He reached to each of us a tiny delicate hand, smiling, nodding, and talking rapidly direct to Allen, familiarly, without waiting for the stilted formalities of the interpreter. The crown prince, clothed like his father but in crimson, was reserved, stolid, trying to pose, I thought, with a haughty and imperious air which he could not maintain and which ill became him. I heard his unfortunate history later, poor man.

I took a great liking to the kindly gentle emperor, so evidently unfitted by temperament and training for the complexities of his rank in a changing civilization, and harried from his early childhood by forces which he did not understand and could not control, but against which he rebelled.

He was born in poverty in a village, the son of a ruined noble of the royal clan, a proud, bitter and scheming man. The boy ran wild with the village children, spun tops with them, flew his kite and lived like any other country boy. News came down to the country of the illness of the childless king. The father hastened up to Seoul, forced his way in to the dying man and by threats and violence drove out the timid eunuchs and palace women from the room. Shortly afterward he came out with great cries of sorrow and announced the king's death to the nobles and ministers of state whose rank did not admit them to the inner chamber, and proclaimed the king's dying wish that, being childless, the country boy should follow him to the throne, with the father as regent to guide him and carry on the government.

It is said that he exhibited a document to this effect signed and sealed by the deceased, but much too long, some whispered who were there, to have been written in so clear and formal a hand in the brief moments of the new regent's conversation with an unconscious and dying man.

The great seal was in his hand. There were ugly rumours later that the king, though dying, had died a little hastily on the arrival of his relative; a trifle sooner, perhaps, than in the course of nature. Still, by Korean rule, possession of the great royal seal carries sovereignty in itself, and there were some sighs of relief that the hated regent had forborne to make himself king. Some did refuse recognition. The powerful Min clan, an older great family and more noble, they claimed, than royalty itself drew off and would not be conciliated nor intimidated. The palace guard submitted to the great seal, a strong argument for the legitimacy of the transaction. The regent, under the title of Tai Won Kun installed himself in the palace, strengthened the guard, drew in new adherents and called upon his reluctant twelve-year-old son to take his place as king and figurehead under his fierce tutelage.

The regent first built himself the great new north palace, and his method of paying for it without funds was characteristic of the man. He comandeered architects, builders, workmen, supplies, and money. Then by edict he ordered that the current copper 'cash' should be received at many times its face value when offered in payment by his men. Refusal carried 'heavy penalty,' and all knew what that meant. When the palace was complete he removed the peg from his currency and it fell to its normal rate.

Peace was bought with the great Mins by offering marriage with the little king to the daughter of their chief, two years older than the boy. Girls in Korea are marriageable at fourteen, and to secure a good alliance are often married much younger. This Min princess was a remarkable woman in every way. She was intelligent and educated, which was a rarity, for Korean women seldom have any education at all, and she was keenly alive to her little husband's interests. A woman of character and unbending will, and a politician far beyond her years and sex, she became from the first a formidable adversary to the regent. She may have been coached by her father, but if so he certainly had good material on which to work. The regent was at first closely allied with the Chinese;

then, after their conclusive defeat by Japan in 1894, he sought the favour of the Tokyo government. The queen worked consistently for her husband's complete independence from restraint and tutelage, and for the independence of Korea from any foreign domination. Men who knew her said that she was not anti-foreign, that she realized the need of government and of adaptation to certain Western things if her country was to survive and live in peace with Western nations, but that she dreaded, in her inexperience, the complications so sure to follow. She did not know how to trust foreign nations. All she wanted was that her country should be free and prosperous and her husband a happy king. Her life was not safe at any moment, and many attempts were made to kill her. Her child husband, terrified by all this violence and intrigue, was an added load. On one occasion their palace was invaded by the regent's men and the king seized. To secure her assassination without responsibility, the gates were thrown open and a drunken mob set on to loot and pillage, so as to cover up her death. Among them rushed in a burly countryman, a miner from the northern province of Peng Yang. Perhaps he was sent by her friends, perhaps he played his own hand. At any rate, he came upon the poor girl in her hiding place, bundled her up in clothes torn from a kitchen-maid, covered her head and face, threw her over his shoulder and strode from the palace gate shouting with obscene jokes that he had got his loot— they might burn the palace now for all he cared. His coarse pleasantries so charmed the regent's guards that they let him pass. He went out swiftly through a broken place in the city wall (all gates were closed and watched, and the queen's friends under guard in their houses) and hid her in a mountain hut. There he convinced her of his loyalty and in due time, when her death had been reported and many people believed it, Ye Yong Ik, her rescuer, revealed her hiding place to her clan, and a counterstoke, supported by the town's people who loved her, relieved the young king and restored her to the palace. Ye Yong Ik became a famous person and stood high at court.

Along toward 1894, whether because of the machinations of the regent or because the Japanese minister at that time was again aiming at annexation and she stood in his way, the queen incurred the mortal enmity of the Japanese legation. According to Korean and even Japanese testimony it was well known that an attempt was to be made to get rid of her once and for all. It was current gossip in the city, and there appears to have been no concealment.

Conferences between the regent and the minister resulted in the arrival of a great number of Japanese officers as military advisers, instructors of the royal guard and company officers replacing Koreans in the regiments. At the same time the Japanese town filled with correspondents and reporters of the Tokyo and Kobe daily papers, who spoke quite openly of what was coming, and with them numbers of those loose fanatical stormy petrels of Japanese politics called soshi, 'strong-arm men,' dressed as students, armed with cudgel or short sword and fed by the political boss to whose side of any controversy they may temporarily adhere. One has heard of gunmen in America protected in some mysterious way. These soshi are a Japanese parallel without the mystery and are ripe for any violence; nor will they 'squeal' when, having accomplished their object, political exigency demands that they be discarded or even sacrificed to exonerate their superior.

In the night of 8 October, 1894, the regent went to the palace of the royal couple, and as the gate was opened to him, a horde of these people, including Japanese officers in Korean disguise, stormed in with him. The queen's guard, composed of tiger hunters and miners from Peng Yang made a moment's gallant defence under their own officers. The king, frantic with alarm and persuaded to yield by his father, the regent, rushed out and ordered them to lay down their arms. Their commander ran in single-handed on the invaders and was cut to pieces. The mob divided, some of them guarding the king and regent, most of them dispersing through the palace shouting for the death of the queen. This time, poor little lady, there was no rough miner to protect her. They found her, cut her down, and threw her, still breathing, on an oil-soaked pile of brushwood, burning her so completely that only a few charred bones were recovered for burial.

The Japanese guard was strengthened in the palace 'for the protection of the king'; the Japanese minister hastened to him to offer his sympathy and remained steadfastly at his side during all audiences given to the rest of the diplomatic corps, who came in to the king as soon as the news spread of what was happening. There were some of the diplomats who suggested that on these occasions their Japanese colleague wore something of the air of a tutelary superior, rather than that of a fellow diplomat accredited to the same sovereign. The king, it seems, was incoherent and unintelligible at these audiences, repeating to each of the foreign diplomats like a lesson learned, his thanks 'for timely Japanese protection,' then breaking down, trembling, weeping, and stammering.

In a few days a proclamation issued from the palace, over the royal seal and the signatures of certain ministers of state known to belong to the Japanese party condemning the queen in contemptuous and insulting terms – to the wild displeasure of the populace, to whom she was a great romantic figure. The people shrewdly guessed that her poor, weak husband had never set his hand willingly to such an insult to her memory. Intercourse with the palace became difficult for foreigners and impossible for natives. A handful of American missionaries braved the displeasure of the winning party and took turns in visiting the king with food prepared by themselves, for he feared poison.

Some time passed and Seoul was startled by a second proclamation, broadcast this time from the Russian legation, extolling the queen's incomparable virtues, lamenting her tragic death and calling on all loyal subjects to avenge it on the persons of her murderers, particularly those Korean ministers who had signed the insulting first edict. The people rose, killed some pro-Japanese officials and dispersed all known to be of that party. The Japanese guard was withdrawn from the palace and the minister, his advisers, officers, reporters and soshi hastily left for Tokyo.

The successful counterplot had been hatched by a serving-woman in the palace. She had continued to go about her kitchen business in the city a dozen times a day, passing the sentries at the gate until they got used to her and grew careless of inspection. That point reached, she took another maid with her, in two box chairs, with renewed vigilance on the part of the sentries followed again by indifference. Then she acted. She left her chair in town, and veiled in the green mantle of the lower people, got access to the Russian legation and the charge d'affaires, and asked him simply if he would receive two highborn guests, with proper military honours. He was quick to see the point. He answered that of course Russian hospitality would never turn away a guest and that any guest would be received with the honour due his rank in the world. The maid then told him, irrelevantly, that she left the palace every day at the same hour with her companion, and that if nothing intervened she would come again to the legation at the same hour next day and hoped that she might be admitted immediately. As at Constantinople, the Russian legation at Seoul kept a guard ship or *stationnaire* in the nearest port, a heavily manned small gunboat, used either for protection or to carry diplomatic mail to the nearest Russian post office. Quite by accident, apparently, just as the maid's chair appeared at the legation next day, a large body of sturdy Russian sailors, fully armed, arrived to take part in a Russian national festival to which the diplomatic corps had been invited. All passed in together, up the hill to where the legation staff stood waiting, and from the carrying chair emerged the king and the crown prince, muffled in women's clothes, and the faithful Om, raised later to high rank for her successful daring.

Safe under Russian protection the second proclamation was issued, and Japanese influence suffered a temporary eclipse. Viscount Miura's coup had been so very bare and so completely at variance with the policy of his predecessor Count Inouye, that European chancelleries asked embarrassing questions and Japanese public opinion was aroused. The government acted, but the party of ruthlessness was still too strong for sober judgment. Viscount Miura and some forty others were placed on trial. One Kunitomo Shigeakira was known to the Japanese residents of Seoul as the murderer of the queen. Together with his brother-in-law Sase Kumatetsu, and Suzuki Junhen (known to Koreans as 'Chokuman' or 'Shorty' Suzuki), he not only boasted of it, but openly received the congratulations of their companions. In general the Japanese colony condemned and deplored in private what they dared not criticize in public. It was proved and admitted at the trial and recorded by the trial judge, Yoshida Yoshihide, in the Hiroshima court that the accused had plotted the violent death of the queen, that they had entered the palace to accomplish their purpose and that Viscount Miura had urged them to kill her; but this curious judicial decision pointed out that there was no evidence to show that 'any of the accused actually committed the crime originally meditated by them.' Witnesses outside the conspirators' party who had seen what had happened were not called, and the corpus

delicti had been destroyed. The Hiroshima court
dismissed the case but the government issued a severe
reprimand to all concerned for harbouring unfriendly
thoughts and intentions, and decreed that officials
among them be deprived of public office. Unlike the
Russian government, which under similar circumstances
transferred M. Hitrovo from the Balkans to Tokyo, the
Japanese government had the good grace to retire their
minister for a while. It was some time before he held
office again, though when it came it was a good one.

The king, safe in the Russian legation, then assumed
the rank and title of emperor, presumably on the feudal
theory that while a mere king may be vassal to an
emperor, an emperor cannot, and that as emperor he
would be the equal of those of China, Japan, and
Russia.

Later came Om's reward. From kitchenmaid she was
raised to the first rank of secondary consorts, to the dis-
gust of the nobles and the delight of the populace, and in
due course became the mother of the monarch's third
son.

Years later, during the beginnings of the Japanese-
Russian war came the final touch of bathos. Those
American war correspondents who had managed to get
through from Tokyo to Seoul (among them Jack London,
who claimed to have crossed in a rowboat) were not
allowed to go to the front and sat kicking their heels with
nothing to report. One of them, representing a great
New York daily undertook to confirm his theory of the
power of the press by creating an incident, developed
under the stimulus of none too good Canadian Club
whisky. He wrote a full page article profusely illustrated,
for his Sunday edition, in which he described the career of
one Emily Brown, a beautiful and virtuous American
missionary, who had so captivated the Korean sovereign
that the emissaries had been sent to negotiate for her fair
hand. The siege was long and the maiden yielded only

when the enamoured king promised his conversion with
that of his whole kingdom to her particular form of
worship. The wedding was performed with great solem-
nity; the American minister (his photograph in oval inset)
gave the bride away; McLeavy Brown and I were official
witnesses, photographs and drawings 'proving' the fact,
and according to this entirely fictitious account Emily,
Koreanized as Lady Om, was now reigning sweetly in
Seoul as royal consort. I have seen this rigmarole restated
in books of reference, and 'Emily Brown,' who never
existed except in a bored correspondent's bravado, has
been listed with Europeans who, like Rajah Brooke,
really have become Oriental potentates.

The Lady Om's son was unquestionably the hope of the
dynasty. His oldest brother, the crown prince, was born
feeble in body and mind, his brave little mother having
submitted before his birth to all kinds of barbarous treat-
ment at the hands of the medicine men and sorcerers,
in order to secure a powerful prince for the succession.
These prenatal efforts as well as his mother's political
hazards and her untimely and savage death wrecked him
in mind and body. His consort was very like his mother, a
clever, eager, intelligent princess, avid of all Western
knowledge.

The second son, born of one of the court ladies, could
never reign. The king was an exemplary husband, according to Oriental customs. Plural marriage, that is legitimacy of official consorts and their sons, was part of the
royal prerogative in all three Eastern empires. There
could be but one empress, but by law a fixed number of
concubines – and outside of the official number there was
still great freedom of choice. Still, the little queen
brooked no rival, and Prince Eui Wha and his mother
were banished in disgrace. As he grew older and the
crown prince remained childless, Eui Wha was taken to
Japan and systematically debauched by a group of conspirators, until through missionaries his father succeeded

in having him removed to America. The cheery little third prince, a sturdy, likable child, though thoroughly petted and spoiled by everybody when he was a baby, has developed under Japanese tutelage better than in all probability anyone could have hoped for him at home. Married to a Japanese princess he also holds Japanese princely rank.

In the Lady Om, our canny miner Ye Yong Ik, the queen's rescuer, found a person whom he could understand. The queen had been grateful to him while she lived, but it was only by the full strength of her will that she could make the court nobles tolerate him. He never bothered with the complicated ceremonial of the court or the etiquette of nobles. He was tall and burly but shambling, dirty and badly dressed, with a sparse, unkempt beard and oozing red eyes. Like 'Diamond Jim' Brady, however, he had an unfallible pass-key to most doors. Brady is supposed to have practised cutting a hundred-dollar bill in two and sending half of it to any obdurate purchasing agent with the message that the other half was waiting outside to join it. Ye Yong Ik collected small nuggets of gold. When he wanted to get in, he sent a little bag of them ahead, but never so far ahead that he could not see what happened to them. With a good many people about the court it worked. With the *nobles de vieille souche* it could not. They despised him utterly, but with them he bided his time.

When Lady Om came to power, he found his way quickly into her good graces. The ambitious miner and the successful kitchenmaid understood each other perfectly. They added to their alliance Kang Sok Ko, the chief eunuch, and through the influence of the two, Ye Yong Ik was made keeper of the privy purse (which covered everything in the kingdom since the king was lord of all), and director of the mint, which was intended to give him in its simplest terms a monopoly of the currency of the country, although that plan went agley.

The coin of the realm was the Chinese 'cash,' a brass or copper piece the size of a quarter dollar, pierced with a square hole in the middle for convenience in stringing them together on a twisted cord in any sum needed. Strings of cash could then be easily loaded across a pony's back for use in any major transaction such as the day's marketing. In order to supply a handier currency, Ye Yonk Ik arranged a concession to an American firm to import blank nickel pieces for his mint, to be turned out to the value of the Japanese five-sen piece. He reckoned without the Japanese, however. No matter how many nickels he stamped and turned out from his mint, he could not compete with the ingenious son of Nippon who placed small and inexpensive hand stamps on the market together with discs of some cheap alloy, with which any man could make his own nickels.

The result was that nobody dared to open the five and ten-dollar rolls in which they came from the mint, lest they turn out to be privately coined and spurious. The rolls were passed from hand to hand as quickly as possible, like 'hunt the ring.' Debts were paid with these rolls with incredible promptness, for everyone was afraid to keep them, so after all no great harm was done to the public.

These three made up the innermost circle of intrigue. Lady Om was no friend to Japan, and had leanings toward Russia, but it was commonly understood that she could be persuaded to take 'a reasonable view.'

Kang Sok Ko, the chief eunuch, was a friend of Allen, and counted as the head of the American party within the palace.

Ye Yong Ik had his way to make, was ready to accept any backing provided it prove the strongest, was counted as leaning toward Russia but was generally credited with being incorruptible, that is, as being a man who would never stay bought.

The three surrounded the emperor with every care, and

it was not often that any communication reached him except through one of them or at least with their knowledge.

All of the court intrigue and much of foreign diplomacy turned on devising new ways of reaching the emperor without their knowledge.

CHAPTER V

CONSULAR COURTS, FOREIGN JURISDICTION AND HIGHER POLITICS

ASIDE from a first-hand study of European diplomacy and Oriental intrigue, an important part of the consular and diplomatic duty of our mission at Seoul was to try high crime and misdemeanour of Americans when we noticed it. There was not often occasion, however, to look up the rules about it in a colony composed of missionaries and business men. With regard to the chief ordinary sources of trouble, merchant seamen coming into Chemulpo were rarely Americans; the navy looks after its own shore parties; communication with the other open ports was intermittent, and the less we knew about them the better.

All foreign consuls were prompt to claim the person of any of their nationals who got into trouble with the native authorities, but few ever made any effort to extend their authority to the prevention of acts by their nationals leading to trouble. Yet the real object of consular courts was to do both things; to protect the native from foreign aggression as well as to protect one's own nationals from native aggression. I hear the system much criticized to-day from lecture platforms by people who do not seem to know very much about how it began, as if it were some violation of the sovereign right of the Asiatic people concerned and an injustice to them of which we ought to be ashamed.

As far as consular courts in eastern Asia are concerned, that war into which England was forced by opium bootleggers, and which led to all our treaties with China, showed plainly enough the danger of allowing large numbers of foreigners to live in countries where they could not in justice be submitted to native law, without supervision of some kind over their acts by their home government.

There is no question at all that foreigners could not be subjected to the laws of Asiatic countries as they were when we first made our present treaties with them, not even criminals. European travellers in eastern Asia in the early Middle Ages did not find that difficulty for a very simple reason: there was practically no difference between their laws and ours, including all the barbarous forms of torture we, as well as they, practised. The difficulty was that Asia still kept those practices which we gradually discarded as we rediscovered Roman jurisprudence and developed our own.

English jurists have pointed out that the system is not, in fact, an extension of foreign jurisdiction to Asiatic soil, but rather a delegation of the sovereign power of an Asiatic government to foreign officials, for the purpose of preventing disorder between two groups of people very wide apart in their manners and customs, to be withdrawn when it is safe for both parties to the agreement to do so.

Whether one takes this English theory as a justification after the event or admits that it is reasonable, the fact remains that some control was necessary over contacts between foreigners and natives for the protection of both; that Asiatics in general were not at that time in a position to exercise it properly, and that foreign exercise of it was often vitiated by the very partnership we complained of in the Asiatic, when no adequate machinery had been set up to insure justice to both.

The tradition of the incompatibility of the East and West, and of some inherent enmity between them, is an age-old thing in Europe, and it was the basis of the whole diplomatic fabric under which we lived in the East. It is a throw-back to the time when the Asiatic was stronger and the European fought for his life against him. If one were to go into far history, it is traceable to the Mediterranean struggle for supremacy in pre-Christian antiquity when Rome grew and became strong, and after the fall of Rome, to the struggle for survival of a nascent Christian Europe against mass invasions from Africa as well as Asia. It was then that the continents hardened into hereditary enemies. The European Christian, not yet wholly Christian nor yet wholly civilized, needed to assert himself strongly and arrogantly against the stronger and superior civilization of the African and Asiatic 'pagan' in order to survive at all.

When Europe, after centuries of development, came back into contact with Asia on the far side of the world, all that ancient arrogance, tinged with an ancient fear, flamed to life again; only, instead of Carl Martel's hammer or the Crusaders' emblems, this time the people of the West carried national prestige and commerce on their banners.

When the United States joined the family of nations, we necessarily took on some of these traditions and procedures. That was in the nature of things. Customs in dealing with Asiatics had been established in the growth of European civilization through the centuries. In theory, however, these same Asiatics made a distinction between us Americans and the European system. In practice, not every Oriental could distinguish between each American and every other foreign devil. Since the average mob could not tell us apart, anti-foreign manifestations included all foreigners, and that forced us into common action in spite of the theoretical distinction between us.

The simple fact is that the consular and mixed courts were set up as a very necessary way of preventing mutual aggression. Too often no proper power was given to do this adequately, and too often where power was granted it was misused.

We all protected our citizens as best we could, but in many cases they were undeniably protected to the exclusion of strict justice to the other side. Then too, whether unconscious of the consequences, or in the interest of national prestige, some diplomats and consuls bustled and blustered about protection where none was necessary, leaving the hopeless feeling in the native that there was no justice against the foreigner, and undoubtedly, too, the growing conviction that since force seemed to be the underlying principle of diplomatic and personal relation with Western foreigners, the Asiatic must learn to meet force with force.

The American legation and consulate exercised their judicial functions in a mildly paternal sort of way like some English squire and justice of the peace, and the convening of an American consular court was an event. Other groups had real and daily use for a much more elaborate and complicated practice, particularly the Japanese, English, and Chinese.

The latter, a numerous and orderly colony, were represented diplomatically by Great Britain, in charge of China's interests – as the American legation was, later, in Panama and elsewhere in South America. In all ordinary matters, however, the Chinese ruled themselves as they do everywhere.

The Japanese body, completely governed from the legation, had nothing to do with anyone else. They had their own administrative organization well served from Tokyo through the minister. In general the Japanese in Korea were disposed, as they are at home, to live peacefully and busily occupied in their own concerns, though not liking the Koreans, nor accepting them as social equals. They lived on reasonably sound business terms with them outside of certain extraordinary and incredibly usurious real estate mortgage operations, which seemed to have the definite purpose of acquiring all the land possible by foreclosure, as well as being highly profitable for those engaged in it. At times, however, the influence of higher politics was distinctly observable in the relations of the Japanese colony to the natives. When the Japanese minister wanted a disturbed condition he could always get it.

It is not going too far afield to note right here that whether in consular courts, diplomacy or business policy, everything that Japan did in China, Manchuria, or Korea shaped toward one end. It is impossible to separate their activities. They were the only ones who, having a definite national policy, carried it out to the last detail.

While Koreans realized the inadequacy of their own legal methods where foreigners were concerned, they resented deeply the undignified position into which their own weakness led them. It is easy to see how far this feeling might reach in other and more powerful countries like China, where similar conditions existed, or Japan, where from the very first modern contacts it was realized that Europe must never be allowed to take the position it had taken in China.

The East felt helpless until they learned something of the physical means of resistance. Present reactions everywhere against manifestations of European personal and national superiority are a direct consequence of its assumption by Europeans as an indisputable fact. Among foreigners generally in the East any foreigner was assumed to be of greater intrinsic value than any native, no matter how convinced we might all be, in the individual case, that it was not so.

I believe that the conviction that force must be met by force has been a reasoned basis of Japanese policy, during the whole of Japan's modern formative period. This conviction was one of the contributory causes of the war with Russia, quite aside from the real menace to Japan of any extension of Russia's power down through the peninsula to within a few hours' distance and almost to within sight of the very heart of Japan. 'A sword aimed at the heart of Japan' was no fantastic simile in connection with what seemed to be Russia's Korean policy. The Japanese themselves have felt that in imitating European ways and methods they momentarily lost the confidence of the other peoples of Asia and, therefore, the possibility of leadership among them. The rest of Asia did not realize, as did Japan, that the superiority claimed for European civilization probably was not an intrinsic property, but rested mainly upon certain governmental, social, and economic theories and upon applied science. The Japanese felt that in mastering these theories and principles they could prove to Asia and to the world that far from being inferior to the European, the Asiatic civilization fortified by the accidental utilitarian advantages of Europe, is really and essentially superior to it. Still, China and India doubted, and argued that theorizing would never prove anything – that proof would lie in successful war. Japan, using Western methods and organization, promptly fought China with over-whelming success. China was not convinced; for the purposes of demonstration of this theory, defeat must be inflicted upon Europeans.

Certain groups in the island empire considered Spain in the Philippines for this purpose. Then came the Spanish-American war, and while it seemed probable to these experimenters in power building that they could dislodge us if they needed to do so, their plans needed to be revised.

In the meantime Russia loomed upon the Korean horizon. Other wars were theoretical. Russia was real and an impending menace. Study of Russia's military position convinced the Japanese that they might succeed, and they realized that if they could win, their position in the world would be unquestioned.

Meanwhile our infrequent appearance as judges was more accidental than designed, and often comic rather than imperialistic.

One case which caused some annoyance and discomfort but more laughter was that of an elderly and unamiable beachcomber, once a citizen of Massachusetts, who kept a wretched longshore shop of damaged groceries and other refuse in the Chinese slum of Chemulpo. One day his death was reported, and a rumour of death by violence, and, as I happened to be vice and deputy consul general in addition to my diplomatic rank, I was sent to Chemulpo to sit as coroner upon him. I had never been a coroner, nor seen one. I had no idea what to do, nor even where to look for the corpse, so I went straight to the centre of all information and community life, the club bar, where I was hailed by the leading citizenry with Rabelaisian laughter and no help. I had heard somewhere of coroner's juries; I did not know what they were, or how they got to be, but I hoped that my ribald mockers would not know either, and in revenge empanelled every American in the club. To my joy, they knew no more about it than I did, and trailed by a complete roster of leading citizens cursing me loudly and bitterly but not daring to refuse to go, I found the lair of the unfortunate subject of the inquest. Everything about it was sordid and disgusting, reeking with filth, and the man himself horridly diseased. Hardy pioneers though they all were, my jury tried to stampede; I was inexorable, threatened impossible and fantastic things and brought them back, though I was obliged to retire myself for a moment. We did examine everything thoroughly and conscientiously, shop and dwelling and body. We corralled an English surgeon, but none of us could find a trace of violence. According to the medical report this dead man's combination of quite evident diseases would be enough to kill anyone. Orientals are reticent in matters of death, but we made among the neighbours as complete an investigation as possible of his habits, his acquaintance, and his movements on the day and night of his death.

The British consul, in charge of Chinese interests and speaking Chinese fluently, helped us, but with nothing to cause the slightest suspicion of violent death, all of which we duly reported back to Seoul.

Meanwhile, his death having been reported by cable (with the addition of the initial rumour) the Department conveyed to the legation the urgent request of the senior senator from Massachusetts that the man's 'murderers be brought to justice.' Senator Lodge was senior senator, and what Senator Lodge wanted any diplomat would make an earnest effort to get for him. Our jury report was not accepted and I was dispatched once more to Chemulpo to find and arrest the murderer, this time as sheriff. The only foreigner connected with the dead man was a nondescript seaman, who had given as satisfactory an account of himself as one expected from a discharged sailor in a rather low seaport town. He was indicated in my instructions, however, as the obvious person to arrest. I found him cleaning and loading a large revolver and explained my mission, requesting him politely to put away his gun and to come along to be tried for murder by our consular court. To my surprise he was quite civil about it. I turned him over to the consul general, and a constable was engaged to keep him in an empty outhouse pending trial. The great day came. At the table in the office sat the court, flanked by Clarence Greathouse, very sleepy, and a missionary, very nervous. All the evidence was produced, including the coroner's report. Evidence is curious matter to handle, as every trial lawyer knows. The man was condemned to death for murder on the same evidence upon which the Chemulpo coroner's jury had decided that there was no possible case against him. Then came the climax. The consular regulations did not extend to the death penalty, as Greathouse woke up long enough to point out.

The consul general, however, was a sportsman. Having no public funds for the purpose, he built a small but costly jail out of his own purse, put in it the prisoner and the newly hired constable and went home to try to straighten out the tangle. Hardly had he sailed before the prisoner walked out and disappeared, but he evidently did not fare as well at liberty as in his snug prison quarters, where the constable cooked for him and talked to him all day, so he returned in a few days. I dismissed the gaoler, put the prisoner on parole (he could not leave the country anyway), let him cook his own meals and made him gardener and stableman until he was transferred to St Quentin in California; and on review of the evidence there, he was released.

A more disagreeable case came up to the French minister. A young French mining engineer in youthful and alcoholic exuberance had forced his way into a Chinese wedding, thereby outraging the wedding guests and starting a formidable riot. He fled to his hotel hotly followed, got a revolver and killed the leading pursuer, who unfortunately proved to be a Chinese head constable, a man of excellent reputation and discretion, who might have arrested him lawfully, but who in his zeal had gone beyond the boundary of the Chinese quarter into the general foreign quarter, where his authority ceased.

Knowing the Frenchman, I was asked for character testimony and could state that under ordinary circumstances, and I had even seen him under trying conditions, he was steady and reliable. He was given the benefit of the *Loi Béranger*, by which in 'crimes of passion' a man's previous character is taken into account, and if good, the sentence is passed but suspended until a second offence. The young man was deported and compensation made to the dead constable's family, with some official exculpation to the Chinese authorities.

The treaty ports, or ports opened by treaty to foreign residence within a three-mile radius of the centre of the town, were governed by several different bodies. The native magistrate had jurisdiction over all Koreans; generally there would be a Japanese concession and a Chinese quarter each under the jurisdiction of its consul, and a general foreign concession under a municipal council composed of all foreign consuls, with the Korean magistrate, the local collector of customs and several leading citizens. Things drifted along very pleasantly under this sytem. In Chinnampo, a small outport, the French collector of customs was also honorary American, French, Russian, British and German vice consul, besides having his personal vote as elected property owner. As colleagues he had a Japanese and a Chinese consul and the native magistrate – three votes in all against his seven. He always had not only a quorum but a majority, except in cases where, under explicit instruction, he might be obliged to vote as American vice consul against himself as Russian, etc.

In Chemulpo things generally ran smoothly. Our whole constabulary consisted of one very old and respectable Chinese night watchman with a huge sleep-dispelling wooden clapper. There was no need for him in the daytime, for nothing ever happened that anybody could do anything about. Foreign residents complained of his noise at night, and so, in solemn session of the municipal council, he was dismissed, and in his place a high-priced 'Jimmie Legs' from the navy was engaged, whose enlistment had just expired. At once we had a most modern crime wave, and no house was safe from robbers. Burglaries took place right under the nose of our constable. Chemulpo had always been a peaceful community; residents complained bitterly, and the council met once more to consider the matter. Next to me sat the

Chinese consul, smiling softly and stroking a thin white beard. I asked him what he thought.

'We are not clever, you know, like you Westerners,' he answered, 'but we think we know the human heart. With us, when a thief goes out to steal he knows that he is sinning and that Heaven is watching him. If, then, he hears the voice of the wooden clapper approaching, it is as the voice of Heaven to his guilty conscience and he flees the spot. The clapper pursues him everywhere. He feels that at any moment justice will overtake him, for someone is watching, even though it be an old and feeble man. Your new constable, alert, young, strong, and well armed is silent. He does not hear the thief and the thief does not know that he is near, so the thief becomes bold. It is not Europeans who are doing these burglaries.'

I voted for the rehabilitation of the ancient one with his wooden clapper – but then, I slept at Seoul, twenty-four miles away. It is true that when we took the Chinese watchman back the crime wave ceased.

Perhaps the Chinese consul was really more clever than the West.

CHAPTER VI

MISSIONARIES

FOREIGNERS in general were restricted to residence in the open ports listed officially for that purpose. Native official eyes were closed to the residence of teachers of the Christian gospel in the interior even when the legality of their being there was doubtful, or its illegality clear.

The reason for their special position went much deeper than treaty agreements; Orientals have a profound respect for all teachers and not least for Christian teachers, for Christianity is Oriental in its origin.

Christianity was introduced to the world, as common property of all the world, under Oriental forms and as the blossoming and full perfection of a religion purely Oriental. Japanese, Chinese, and Korean thinkers have assured me that to the Oriental mind there is not only no difficulty whatever in Christianity but that it is all marvellously simple to them, and that obstacles to its reception as elsewhere, are not inherent in the Christian religion but in the materialism which has incrusted it, in the 'fact that Westerners have not understood Christianity and prove it by their mutual divergence and animosities; by their insistence on making Christianity a vehicle for the furtherance of their political views and the advancement of their national ambitions,' and, finally, in the 'impertinence of Westerners attempting to explain an Oriental message to Orientals' anyway, even if they had understood it themselves.

That is not as superficial nor as egotistical as many excellent and sincere Western Christians set it down to be. There is a good measure of truth in it as there is even in the sectarian discords among Christians themselves.

It has always seemed to me to be possible and advantageous to mission work to find first the common ground, accept that, and build upon it, urbanely, logically and, therefore, convincingly. Except in rare cases that has not been the practice in those parts of the East in which I have experience.

The Oriental who has known Buddhism is perfectly familiar with several aspects of Catholic religious life, such as asceticism, contemplation, ritual, and rubric, the monastic life and even sacerdotalism. The Catholic priests and nuns who conducted the first Asiatic missions and introduced Christianity are perfectly intelligible to the East. So too, is the healthy family life and benevolent humanitarianism of the protestant medical missionary, and when it is a question of American mission workers, there is sympathy for and understanding of their views on politics, the political state and social justice.

It may be questioned in all sobriety, however, if in these latter the Oriental does see the fullest teaching of Christianity, or, conversely, whether at all times he sees in the former the aloofness from temporal interests which the perfection of Christianity should carry with it. What he thinks he sees is the tying in of spiritual work to the interests of some political power. He sees nationality in apostles; he sees mission work protected by gunboats, perhaps unavoidably, perhaps justifiably, but very really whether justifiable or not. He recognizes the spiritual ardour of many and the perfect readiness for possible martyrdom, but behind it he sees Western government ever ready to cover the apostle with the mantle of the national citizen or subject, and to exact posthumous satisfaction in money or in political spheres of influence wrested from the native government which failed to protect the victim of blind mob vengeance on the nearest foreign devil for some real or fancied aggression or injustice on the part of some foreign government.

That is obviously a difficult problem for political government to solve. To leave missionaries unprotected, alone of all citizens or subjects, might easily mean to expose them to any ebullition of the lawless. To protect them exposes their spiritual mission to the reproach of prostitution to political ends. The solution lies, of course, in the erection of native churches, of native hierarchy, clergy, or other church forms at the earliest possible moment. It has long been debated among mission boards whether this is a safe thing to do. That, if one might hazard a guess, depends largely upon the divine origin of Christianity. What is divine must stand, in the logic of things.

In Korea the two principal mission bodies were French Catholics and American Evangelicals. The French had come in from China, in very early days, smuggled across the borders of the Hermit Kingdom, when discovery of a foreigner meant death under the law. Their coming, in spite of almost certain death, was connected with the fact that a body of Catholic Christians existed there already, without the direct action of missionaries. Korea was in some loose degree dependent upon China during centuries. Up to the victory of Japan over China, Korean embassies visited annually the court of Peking, and much of the Chinese learning passed down to the Korean capital in this manner. These embassies brought back with them fashions, books of science, the newest in art and literature, everything of cultural value which China might receive through wider contact with the world. Among other curiosities of current literature several books were bought in expounding a new religious doctrine: Christianity, which had arrived in China through Francis Xavier and his companions. Numbers of men of the noble and educated class sought eagerly for more, and in

1784 dispatched one of their number to obtain it. He became a Christian, was baptized and on his return baptized many more. In 1791 several of them were executed for refusing the traditional sacrifice. In 1794 a Chinese priest was sent in to them and discovered some four thousand Catholic Christians. In 1836 French priests followed, with great secrecy, since Christianity had been officially proscribed. In 1839 a new persecution broke out. The French bishop Monsignor Imbert, believing the movement to be anti-foreign rather than anti-Christian, sent directions to his priests, as soon as he was arrested to give themselves up in order to save their people. They all responded to the call and were executed. After that date the country remained firmly closed and Christianity more completely proscribed than ever, but in spite of it French missionaries continued to enter, being ordinarily transferred at sea from Chinese junks to Korean fishing boats. In 1863 the mission counted 25,000, two bishops and ten missionaries. A persecution in that year wiped out the French clergy with the exception of three, who returned to China. A French naval expedition, sent to protect them, accomplished nothing but a severe slaughter on the mud flats of Kangwha Island, the fortress at the mouth of the Han, on whose banks Seoul is placed, seventy-five miles up the river. In 1876 a new attempt was made to revive the mission; the new bishop was arrested, but released on the demand of the French minister at Peking and expelled from the country.

Religious liberty came, however, with the commercial treaties of 1884. An American naval squadron after severe fighting at Kangwha inflicted a complete defeat upon the Korean forces in 1871, but the object of both the French and American naval expeditions remained confused in the minds of Koreans, and in spite of their losses they believed that they had beaten off two Western fleets.

With the opening of Korea by commerical treaties and

reasonable security for teachers of religion, the French
settled openly, and new missions arrived principally from
America. Hospitals, orphanages, asylums for old people,
schools and mission stations sprang up all over the country,
in or near all the principal towns. So vigorous was the
activity of American medical missionaries that soon all
Americans travelling in the back lands were assumed by
the country people to be physicians, and no one could
escape trying his hand at simple cures.

All Americans were missionaries to them, and all
missionaries were men of science. Now, that is an
excellent basis upon which to build mission effort, and
many of the medical missionaries merited the popular
conception of their powers. All known diseases and many
then unknown in the West were prevalent. Any physician
could get more practice in his daily life than he possibly
could at home, and they did not spare themselves. Old
Hippocrates never had more loyal and devoted disciples.

Koreans from the American mission schools were
active in government reform. There was a major difference in the methods of the Americans and the French
engaged in mission work, and both have been reproached
for their systems. The French priests were primarily
interested in the Christianity of their people. They were
not interested in Westernizing them nor in making them
expert even in a Western language. On the contrary they
conformed as nearly as possible themselves to native customs and in many instances had nearly forgotten their
own tongue. Their schools were largely orphanages,
where children were brought up as Christians and
married to each other at maturity to found new Christian
families. They were often set down, therefore, by other
Western people as obscurantists, doing nothing for the
civilization of their people.

American missions, on the other hand, conducted hospitals and schools in which not only Western knowledge
was taught, but natives were Westernized and liberalized

to such a degree that they were to be found in every liberal reform movement, which at that time was synonymous in Korea with rebellion and revolution.

The nationalist party which caused some degree of anxiety to the Japanese annexation movement had in it men from these schools.

Consequently, just as the French were set down by some as obscurantists, so were American missions set down as hotbeds of revolution and Westernization of the native.

Neither is a legitimate reproach. It is unthinkable that Americans, mainly from our small towns and all quite '100 per cent' and over, could possibly have anything in common with the irregularities of native government. They must inevitably protest against it and thus react upon the native reformer. Both the American and the French systems seemed entirely respectable. Yet, just as American missionaries did lay the foundations of the various liberal movements, it is undeniable also that French national 'prestige' was greatly enhanced by the fact that even at the height of the anti-clerical movement in France, when priests and nuns were being expelled or laicized, the French legation staff never failed to attend French cathedral ceremonies in full uniform, whenever it was good publicity to do so in the interest of France.

There were certainly men in both principal mission bodies whose zeal was embarrassing to their diplomatic representatives and to foreign administrators in the civil government. When it comes to religious disputes, the civil administrator is likely to find himself in the uncomfortable rôle of Pilate. Never till I lived in a primitive mission country did I understand Pontius Pilate as perhaps not the cynical, damned traitor he is painted, but rather as an alien career administrator of a mandated territory, a politician whose sole object was to keep the peace, not to govern. He has always been a type most common in diplomacy and in colonial administration, the patron saint of the career man.

Conflict between missionaries and local magistrates seemed inevitable. The missionary lived outside of places open to foreign residence. Nobody minded his living there, but no native official would dare to interfere with anything he did, even if he wished to do so. Conscious of that, some missionary would often assume for himself a semi-diplomatic status and would usually extend the same privilege to the natives who formed part of his household, as teachers, catechists, or servants. His house would thus assume by custom the status of an embassy; a further step would make it an asylum for anyone taking refuge there, and finally, exemption from the jurisdiction of the magistrate would be assumed for all native Christians of that mission. That is quite possibly the way bishops' courts started in early Christianity at Rome, to be confirmed later by Roman law, but in Korea it had a disconcerting consequence. All kinds of loose fish would join up in a mission because of the protection it gave. The native magistrates were not all competent officials and were far from being all honest. Clashes became almost unavoidable.

When a native Christian claimed his pastor's protection against official extortion there was, unfortunately, too often a chance of truth in it. There was also too often a chance that some rascal was escaping native justice by sheltering in the pastor's fold. Those were difficult cases to handle.

Equally difficult were the cases of burning zeal such as that of the missionary who was determined to end devil worship in his community and cut down a superb tree, the abode of a village tutelary spirit, which covered the market place with its branches. Most difficult of all were the quarrels of two rival pastors and their flocks, of different nationality as well as conflicting theological views.

Nothing ever equalled the joy with which their native Christians sailed into each other with clubs and stone slings. One had a complete picture in miniature of the religious wars of Europe, with the village scallawags thumping each other heartily in the cause of rival clergymen, for the sake of the particular side on which the butter was spread for them. The Korean magistrates were utterly helpless and only hoped that nothing of it would come to the ears of high officials at the capital, or worse, to the foreign legations, for it was all more than likely to come back on the local native official in the end.

Another source of trouble came from the very fact that surrounded by a primitive culture Americans were trying to live American lives as nearly as possible and thereby came into conflict with conditions governing the business conducted by other Americans in the open ports.

Among commercial men at the treaty ports, most of whom lived by agencies for various exporters at home, American missionaries had a bad name, first because they lived with impunity outside of the treaty limits of foreign residence, which business men could not do; and secondly, because, living as they did, with their families, it was necessary for them to live as nearly as possible as they would at home. Consequently they would bring out for their own use every labour-saving appliance or agricultural implement they could afford to have, all of which were of immense interest in the natives. Having learned the use of them, natives wanted them, and it was a simple matter for the missionary to send home to some mail order house for them, never thinking, probably, that he thereby deprived the merchant in the port of his agency commission. More than likely, orders for things wanted in the interior and useless in the ports would bring inquiry to the agent pertinent to the transfer of his agency to someone who could sell – a missionary for

instance – which in turn would call forth bitter, and rather
unreasonable, condemnation of missionaries in general,
by the merchants. All that was trying to officials, native
and foreign; upsetting to the magnificent work the
majority of the missioners were doing in many lines;
irritating to the Koreans generally and very damaging to
the cause of religion. One narrow theologian, crabbed
and ignorant bigot or tactless zealot, can do more damage
than a dozen saints can overcome in a lifetime.

Fortunately the majority of American evangelical
missionaries were exceptionally fine people. It never
seemed to me out of keeping that they had their social
club and tennis courts and their good American gather-
ings there on Thanksgiving Day and at Christmas. Most
of the foreign officials in Seoul were bachelors or had not
brought out their wives. It was a great relief to get out of
bachelor parties into the family circle of the missionary
groups, even those which looked upon the card playing
and cocktails, the horse racing and dancing, of the official
lot as next door to the seven deadly sins.

Arthur Turner, later Anglican bishop of Korea, did not
go quite that far though he certainly thought we all had
far too much time on our hands not to be doing something more serious with it. He was a famous athlete, and it
was told of him that he once fought out a conversion with
his fists in his first curacy in some mining village in
England. It was not at all a godly village apparently, a
most unlovely one in fact. A group of young bullies
decided to put him out of it, led by a great hulking fellow
who had never been thrashed. They tried various ways of
making Turner's life miserable and then when that failed
tried to intimidate him. Finally, the leader of the gang
struck him. Turner said to them very quietly: 'You don't
want me here, but I would not go if I could, and I can't
anyway, for I am under orders. We can't go on this way, so
I suggest we fight it out. You pick your man and if I win

you will take orders from me. If I lose, we will try it all over again until I win.' He won. It may not be true, but it sounds very like him.

There was a time when we all got badly on each other's nerves in the younger crowd. Turner made up his mind that it had gone far enough, invited us all to meet at my house and brought a couple of sets of singlesticks with wicker helmets. He then ordered us to strip to the waist and lay on in couples, in the broiling sun while he sat on the veranda and smoked. None of us knew how to use the infernal things, so the carnage was dreadful, but after he had tied us up and put compresses on and fed us Scotch and cigarettes (both mine) I am sure we all felt better, even spiritually.

I have suggested already that it was never quite clear to me that Koreans really sought Christianity of American missions. It seemed that what they saw there was a humanitarian ethical life, political principles which appealed to many strongly, and a simple access to knowledge of Western life which they wanted and needed, but that all that life did not mean to them religion. There is a mystical content in religion, to the Oriental mind; together with that mysticism goes a perfect comprehension of the idea of religious authority. Asiatics everywhere have rebelled in past centuries against priestly domination in politics, but the priestly and even monastic function are well defined in their minds. Atonement and penance for sin are a commonplace to them, as is vicarious atonement. The custom of the scapegoat loaded with the sins of the people was current in Korea in my time, in national emergency such as cholera epidemics. Many Hebraic customs and items of the Mosaic law are part of their lives. They might, in fact, be easily brought to Judaism, but Judaism being the root of Christianity, so might they easily be brought to that interpretation of Christianity which is most consonant with the austerity and contemplative mysticism which so fascinates the Oriental mind. Religion and occidental learning, it seemed to me, were two separate and distinct things, and often, acceptance of religion meant to Koreans (as I think to Chinese also) acceptance merely of a Western standard of ethics not incompatible with their own, upon which to ride to Western knowledge as upon some convenient vehicle. I would have liked to see their reaction to Francis of Assisi, or to some of the great contemplative mystics, uncomplicated by nationalism, electric railroads, telephones, and political theories.

I do not hold at all with those who consider Western missionary activity futile or injurious. On the contrary, the great-hearted men and women who have carried to them their sincere convictions have revolutionized the Korean's attitude toward foreigners in general, and, in spite of sectarian discords, these convictions have altered the Korean doubt that Europeans really do believe in Christianity. Many are inclined to think that the Western mind does not, and perhaps cannot, wholly assimilate it, but many thoughtful Orientals also do respect their various attempts.

In missionary matters the State, through diplomacy, is forced into situations concerning the Church, through activities of ministers of the gospel, wherever the State must take cognizance of the status of all its citizens or subjects.

That is a question which must be solved at home before it is carried abroad under the missionary's mandate, to 'go, teach all peoples.'

CHAPTER VII

LIFE IN THE LEGATIONS

THE American legation was one of the most comfortable in Seoul. The Russian, French and Japanese legations and the British consulate general were of that cheerless type of imitation European house built by a Japanese or Chinese contractor. All the others were Korean bungalows made over, and the Korean style lends itself very well to remodelling. They are well raised from the ground on a granite block foundation. The mud or brick walls are weatherproof, and the ceiling, supported by heavy oak or chestnut beams, is covered with tons of packed earth rising to a high roof ridge, on which clay tiles are laid, so that neither summer heat nor winter cold strikes through.

The double gates of our legation under a tower roof, rather like a castle gate, opened onto the missionaries' tennis courts, just along the entrances to the British compound and the emperor's new palace. On either side of the gate was a guardroom for the kisu, or gatemen, dressed in mediaeval native soldiers' uniform, who with the chair-bearers and rickshaw runners were supposed to be always on duty at the gates, day and night. To the right on entering was a half courtyard of one-storey storehouses, made over into barracks for a marine guard which was stationed there once in a while from the Asiatic squadron, though I do not think we ever actually needed one. Next to that was the office quadrangle, then a broad lawn and the big, rambling house occupied by the minister and his family. My road led up from the left of the main entrance, between the minister's servants' quarters and the outer enclosure to another gate at the top of a short flight of steps giving access to a charming garden shaded by deodars, and filled with great peony bushes and azaleas. Beyond was another wide lawn, surrounded on three sides by narrow terraces built of granite blocks, with chrysanthemums and iris and flowering shrubs rising to a ridge crowned with trees and enclosed by a high wall. Between the garden and the lawn lay my bungalow, just two living-rooms, a bedroom and a dining-room with kitchen and servants' quarters. In winter one American Round Oak stove kept the whole house comfortable though it might be thirty to forty degrees below zero outside, and in summer it opened out under the wide eaves to the trees and flowers. The privacy of a sunken lawn surrounded by flowers and filled with dickey birds was irresistible. I used to have the Chinese boy set my tin bathtub in the middle of it in springtime until one morning I heard voices that I recognized behind me, then several feminine squeaks followed by frozen silence. A lady who had once occupied my bungalow and loved it had brought friends 'from the States' who were visiting her to see my flowers, thinking I was out of town, and had come in through a little postern gate in the wall. I pretended to be unconscious of them, but did not linger after they had slammed my gate. While I was still wondering from whom an apology was due, if it was, a note came in from the lady's husband rebuking me for my immoral conduct. These were the Victorian days.

Life was easy at Seoul. One kept far too many servants, according to the custom everywhere in the East. There must be a head boy and a second boy and a coolie for the housework even in a bungalow of four rooms. The two first must be Chinese; the coolie might be a native. His job was the heavy cleaning and polishing of floors, walls, roof beams, and everything in the house capable of being made to shine. When he was not busy at that, he moulded balls of soft coal dust and wet clay and baked them in the sun all summer for the stove, where they glowed with much heat and no flame into white powdery ash. A Chinese cook and scullion were necessary even for the needs of one bachelor who only dined at home when people dined with him. Then there must be a private rickshaw runner, a gardener and a groom for the horse. When one went abroad officially one took the kisu and chair-bearers from the guardroom.

The head boy and the cook were colleagues and equal, each chief in his own sphere, with a slight advantage to the head boy (or number one boy, in pidgin English) who was treasurer and paymaster of the household. These two functionaries expected to put aside their whole wages every month and to make enough from bonuses and pickings to double them. That was an eternal cause of disorder in any house where the bachelor master took to himself a wife straight from home. No woman coming out for the first time ever understood why we put up with that system and always started out like a good housekeeper to break it up. The point is that the head boy and the cook, according to immemorial custom, are the housekeepers between them. The pickings of honest servants are limited rigidly to one hundred per cent of their wages, and no one else is allowed to get at your purse in any way. They are the most jealous watchdogs of your expenses that could be. They shave every grocery bill or any other, beyond the percentage of it which is their due from the shopkeeper or contractor. You know that when you engage them for so much a month they mean and you mean double that, but if you get honest ones, you are perfectly safe from all other birds of prey.

Both these house positions are more or less hereditary. That is, a head boy chooses his own assistant as second boy. You have nothing to do with that. He proposes a likely boy and you accept, since you have nothing to do with him anyway. You give house orders only to the head.

The second boy will always be a young relative of number one, under his training and professional guidance. Some day or other number one will come and tell you he must go back to China. You know then that number two is considered adequate to take charge and is to be promoted, while a new junior member of the family appears to take his place.

If you entertain frequently the cook becomes an important person and head of a school. Innumerable young Chinese fill your kitchen, who pay your cook a monthly sum for the privilege of learning under him. Anything that is spoiled or broken in the process the cook replaces – and if you should ever hear sounds of anguish from the kitchen (a grave breach of etiquette) you may mention the fact of indecorum to number one boy, but you may not inquire what has happened. You know that someone is being taught with a broom handle not to spoil your food or break your crockery, and after all, these apprentices are not your servants and cost you nothing. These cooking schools in your house are very serious affairs. The first Englishmen, Frenchmen, Germans, and Russians in the East took great pains to train up good cooks and teach them their favourite national dishes, or they brought out first-class foreign cooks to legations and hongs who trained the Chinese. Each one of the Chinese cooks then set up his own school and trained others to the exact process he had learned. If you were particular, you asked a cook's professional pedigree as you would learn that of a racing two-year-old.

House servants have a higher status than others and must be treated with reserve. They may not be scolded, nor spoken to abruptly. You keep your own dignity and respect theirs.

In Peking, house servants in a noble's house or in some legations had even a small official rank. Curiously enough they were nearly all Catholics, of the old stock first con-

verted by Francis Xavier's companions. These men are
very neat and careful in their dress; immaculate blue or
white cotton for ordinary occasions, and beautiful
brocades for formal ones. They take great pride in your
house, and are quick to think of your needs.

In a community of bachelors, it often happened that a
half-dozen or more men at the club would decide to dine
with one of the number and a message would go to his
cook, with the names of the guests. Probably the cook
would not have enough food in the house, but that never
mattered. On arriving each guest would find his own boy
there with something from his own kitchen or wine-room
specified by the host's cook. If on the spur of the moment
the whole company decided to stay where they were and
not bother to go home, each house boy arrived the next
morning with fresh linen and other clothes and all
necessary minor things, each with a coolie bearing his
master's tin bathtup.

For rickshaw coolie one preferred a Japanese, for they
were neater than the natives and far better runners than
Chinese or Koreans. I had an excellent and devoted man,
though I did not realize that it was undignified for him to
do that work outside of Japan. Because I could make
myself understood to him in his own language he treated
me in all things as though I were a Japanese, and took my
word as he would have done under the old clan system at
home. He came to me one day to tell me that he must kill
his wife, as was his right. That he could not do that while
in my service, so he must leave me. I asked if he realized
how greatly that would inconvenience me, and forbade
him either to kill his wife or to leave my service. There
was no use at all in taking it any other way. He accepted
my decision. This man also took care of a very fine horse I
bought from the commander of the Japanese guard.
'Maedzuru' (Flying Crane) had been cross bred from
several Arab horses sent by Napoleon III as a present to
the Japanese emperor. There was no horse like him in

Korea, and I was very careful of him. One day I was taking a short cut over a piece of ground occupied by a very small Polish squatter and his very large and powerful Russian peasant wife. The lady seemed to be in a nervous state about something, for she picked up a pitchfork and lunged at poor Maedzuru with it as I passed. I just avoided losing a good horse by a wheel that would have been passable in a rodeo, and since the sudden attack had got him startled, I let him go. I heard queer sounds behind me and as soon as I could pull up, came back to find my Japanese strangling the woman. I suggested that in our customs we did not choke women to death.

'But,' he said, 'she raised her hand against the master – and besides she doesn't look like a woman, and when she strikes she doesn't feel like one.'

The native servants were neither as competent as the Chinese and Japanese, nor of equal social rank. The gatemen, chair-bearers and guards were a continual source of trouble. Unlike Japan, where maidservants are usual, in Korea as in China one has only men for servants, and all classes were inveterate gamblers. The Chinese and Japanese managed their dissipations among themselves, with rarely a scandal, but the Korean servants could not be left to themselves. They had to be ruled.

I was once informed by the governor of the city that our legation native servants had become a public scandal, for relying on the immunities of a diplomatic household, they had made their quarters a public gambling place, and the city police could not reach them. No warning from me had any effect on the hardened sinners, so I asked the governor what to do about it. If I let his police arrest them it would be a bad precedent and besides I would have to get others who would be no better.

'I know what any Korean would do,' he said, 'but probably a foreigner would be too squeamish about it.'

'Well?'

'About once every few months, we know our people are

out of hand, though we may not be able to fasten anything on any individual, and it would be fatal to try to do
it, for they would all have perfect alibis. When that
happens we call them all up one morning, have the headman give each a good, well-cut stick, and order them to
switch each other's tails thoroughly. Of course, the master
has to sit there to see that they aren't too polite about it
to each other.'

'Do they do it?'

'Certainly. They all know of some secret sin, and if you
don't specify, they think you do too. In your case they all
know they are guilty. If they do it thoroughly it clears the
atmosphere for quite a time.'

Not being squeamish, I ordered them all up on the
lawn, having got a very effective bundle of switches, and
had my chair placed on the grass, with a table beside it, as
solemn as a high court of justice. One look at the switches
and they all knew what was coming. I handed the headman a switch and told him to begin where he liked. He
took it, bowed, and walked over to the nearest man. Both
bowed and the headman apologized for what he was
about to do. The victim begged him not to mention it and
modestly lowered his baggy trousers sufficiently. Ten
vigorous strokes, and the executioner looked at me.

'For an example and a foretaste, it may be enough,'
I said.

Both bowed to each other and to me, and the victim
took a fresh switch and went through the same perform-
ance with the next, now taking the ten strokes for granted,
but each repeating the same thing like a ritual of
etiquette. The last man gave the headman his; all bowed
to me and waited to be dismissed. They knew perfectly
well that I had been coached in native customs, probably
by my friend the governor, and that it would be unsafe to
try anything more. After that they kept their gambling to
themselves. The story shocked my American missionary
friends, but after all Fr Arthur Turner the future bishop

had once done the same thing to us junior diplomats, with single-sticks, for reasons awfully like mine.

Some of these men are extraordinarily skilful with flowers. They do not grow beds of flowers except as seed beds on the narrow granite terraces which surround a city garden. Out of these seed beds of iris or chrysanthemums they select several perfect plants, pot them at just the right time in the great ornamental jars the Japanese make, and give all their care to these, to be a credit to the master on a given date. Chrysanthemums, being the flower of the emperor of Japan, were due on the third of November. In the late summer slips were taken from the best plants of different kinds and colours, and transplanted several times, until the final potting. Generally only the top bud was allowed to remain, so that all the strength of the plant and all the gardener's care would go to make one perfect flower. Though the special date was Japanese the chrysanthemum custom prevailed everywhere in the north of Asia.

That garden bungalow was the most attractive place I had in the East and one of the most charming I have had in all my wandering in far places. There is a peace in a Korean garden such as I do not know in any other part of the world. It is not silence, for the clear air is full of voices; there are birds all about in the trees and bushes, magpies on the roof and always kites swinging in the sky, whistling to each other. It is a perfect calm over everything, the sort of thing you get from the Irish legends of the land of the Shee or the holy places.

I was sorry to leave it when I changed from the legation of the palace.

It was in this little bungalow I had an adventure with Prince Henry of Prussia. The prince had come out on his famous visit to the East, just after the Kaiser's equally famous speech about the 'Mailed Fist.' We did not know then what it was all about. To-day it seems clear that the emperor had suddenly realized that England and Japan,

France and Russia were about to devour the choicest sections of Asia, just as the powers had partitioned Africa, and that if that was to be, Germany might find herself at considerable disadvantage for industrial markets. Since none of the four appeared to have any regard for anything but force, it probably seemed to him necessary to remind the East rather forcibly that Germany must not be disregarded, if their possessions were to be simply handed out. Of course, any powerful nation playing for high stakes in world trade would have found it far better policy to make friends with the East, for Asia badly needed a friend; but that need not be criticized at this late date. We did not know it then and we have all seen where that aggressive policy led, which everybody pursued, not Germany alone.

Prince Henry seemed to be thoroughly imbued with the spirit of Walter Scott's French knight, who seated himself on the Greek emperor's throne to show his independence. He was naturally a charming gentleman, but in the East he was rough, and instead of impressing the Koreans he filled them with amazement. Still, that too is neither here nor there. It was all a pose and a mistaken policy, in full accord with what all the other European powers were doing.

We made our ceremonial calls, of course, at the German consulate, and the prince made court circle for the diplomats. Later he sent me word that he wished to call on a famous Dutch artist and his wife who were staying with me, that he would like to spend the afternoon quietly, without ceremony and without being entertained – unless, as he added jovially, I had any real German beer. I did have some, and sent my horse for him to ride over. We had a charming afternoon. He stayed till almost dinner time, in spite of reminders from the gentleman of his staff who came with him. His conversation was a delight, and he was kindly, informal, and homely in the real German way. As we went out to where the horse was waiting for him, he suddenly drew himself up very straight, went red in the face, glared at me and said:

'I hope you understand clearly that I was calling on my Holland friends and not at the American legation nor on you.'

I am afraid I lost my temper, as diplomats ought never to do with royalty, and I answered, in the same German we had been using most amiably all the afternoon that I had understood the situation perfectly, had endeavoured to meet his wishes and now thought him quite unprovokedly discourteous. He raised his hand as if to strike me and I lunged forward to lay him out before taking a blow, but an international scandal was prevented most providentially by his naval aide, a delightful person, Capt Karl von Müller, who was, I think, the same who later commanded one of Germany's most successful surface sea raiders, the *Emden* – a sailor who won the complete respect and personal friendship of every English sailor who was after him. He seized the prince's arm, threw me an anguished 'Um Gottes Willen, Herr Sands!' and fairly hustled him on to my horse. My poor Maedzuru was spurred as he never had been spurred before and bucked his way across the legation lawn down to the gate and to the German consulate in a cloud of dust and Koreans flying for their lives.

I cannot imagine what got into Prince Henry to make him spoil a perfect afternoon, unless a belated memory of the Mailed Fist mission. Still, he did not need to try that on me. I knew Germany very well, and German customs, and had remembered my manners prettily all the afternoon, according to the German rules of the game. I rather dislike to tell the story now, except as an illustration of those things every foreigner was doing to make his particular nation disliked by other Europeans and Asiatics as well, and to prepare for the general smash which came fifteen years later, all in the belief that they were increasing peoples' respect for them.

The Koreans were full of such incidents of Prince
Henry's visit. One more is enough to show the tactless-
ness of Western diplomacy. About a year later I was on
duty in the palace when I heard a most indecorous noise
in my courtyard; a heavy running, the scolding of
eunuchs and little squeals of some child's laughter. I
suspected the baby prince, the Lady Om's son, who was a
privileged character. Into the room burst the emperor's
uncle, the 'Fat Prince,' panting and perspiring and gasp-
ing 'that child will be the death of me,' and after him the
baby with a cat in his arms and a flock of disturbed palace
eunuchs. I knew the Fat Prince's weakness, an aversion to
cats so strong that they made him ill. I had seen him faint
once at dinner at the legation because of a kitten hidden
behind a curtain, which he could not see, but felt to be
there. After I had got rid of his tormentor and calmed the
old gentleman down, he said he had been on his way to see
me because he knew that I was his friend and a most
valued friend, and he wanted to do something very special
for me. I wondered what next, for he was an unusual
old party.

'You American men, who have no king of your own,
like kings and princes, nevertheless. Perhaps it is because
you all claim to be something like kings yourselves, and
like to claim equality with kings. I have heard that it is
so.'

Still I wondered.

'Now I am a royal prince, and the uncle of an emperor.
A royal prince and brother of one of the greatest
emperors in the world (as I am assured) came to Korea
last year, and after he went away, he sent me the most
valuable present he could find to remember him by, an
imperial gift from one royal prince to another. That is the
present I have brought you, as the most perfect thing I
can give you,' and he handed me an American watch
which sold at that time for ten dollars.

Prince Henry's present to the Korean general who had

acted as his aide was a cheap .32 calibre Smith and
Wesson revolver, and his present to the emperor himself
was a carved wooden cuckoo clock such as hangs in every
peasant's house in the Harz Mountains.

My friend the Fat Prince, to judge from his over-
elaborate politeness, was very angry about it. The
Koreans had done their level best to entertain Prince
Henry and spent more money on it than they had any
right to spend. They had hoped that, since Germany
belonged neither to the Russian-French alliance nor to
the Anglo-Japanese group, they might find a friend and
protector in the Kaiser to prevent their spoliation by
either. It was Germany's chance to be friendly and disinterested in the scramble for territory and to profit
thereby enormously in trade, but then no one could see
far even into the future as we are to-day, and nobody
could foresee a time when diplomacy unbacked by a
rather contemptuous gesture of force would be worth
trying.

If our days were not strenuous in the legations, neither
were they idle. Home mail came about once a month;
sometimes one had letters not much over a month old.
American daily newspapers for that reason were of no use
at all, though missionaries in the interior fell on them
greedily. State Department instructions were read leisurely
the first week and answered or acknowledged during the
following three if one were methodical, or if one were
otherwise occupied, on the day and night before the
steamer sailed. There were several routine things to be
done like annual reports, one report every six months, a
quarterly report or two and a regular statement of pay
drafts, which we drew on a London bank, since our own
banks were not known outside of the village of New
York. The half-yearly report had to do, I think I remember,
with the War Department's property in Seoul, a dozen
ancient Springfield single-shot rifles, of the earliest vin-
tage, which had been allotted to us in former days for the

defence of the legation, with several hundred rounds of mouldy cartridges. After getting off a couple of reports on their condition it occurred to me that one could not really know, if one had never tried them. It would also be interesting to find out whether cartridges expended would ever be replaced by the War Department. Also, if one expended prehistoric ammunition which was no longer made, how the various branches of the government would go about the business of restocking us. I saw possibility of a lively correspondence lasting over years, and decided to try it. The opportunity came with a Japanese innkeeper who kept the half-way house on the road to Chemulpo where everybody stopped for lunch. He came in one morning to announce that a tiger had been about the place and asked me to come down. I got a mining engineer to go with me and we took two long Springfields and a pocketful of cartridges apiece. We borrowed a small pig from the innkeeper and since the whole country is wide and bare at the spot decided to lie out on a small grassy hill that night under a gorgeous autumn moon. The tiger had been there; the track was plain enough, so we tethered the pig some distance down where he had passed, and tied a long cord to his hind leg. One of us was to pull the cord and make the pig squeal while the other man slept. Some time after midnight, in my turn to watch, I saw a movement down the valley; something moving toward the sound of the pig. Allowing everything I could think of for the vagaries of moonlight, I adjusted my sights on a guess and waited till the tiger should come out from a dark patch into a brilliantly lighted spot beyond, when suddenly the long quaver of a Chinese song arose from the dark patch and I dropped the muzzle of my rifle while a Chinese pedlar walked out into the spot I had covered. The next morning we tried all our cartridges, but not one would fire.

I have since heard Mexicans make the same comment about our government ammunition sent down to help them suppress a revolution. It was just as well that Korean tigers rarely appear twice in the same place and travel far between stops. I tried to make a report on it for the War Department but decided that it would not look at all interesting to them even though unaccompanied by an expense account for the official test.

Acknowledging quite dull and uninspired instructions was easy. It was much harder to invent a subject for a dispatch that had not been said a million times before. On those rare and happy occasions when all the legation chiefs were away except the Japanese minister, who never slept and never went away, various junior secretaries would pool their secrets and try to work out an identical dispatch to all the European chancelleries and the Washington government. It never amounted to anything nearly as exciting as that of the German consul when the emperor escaped to the Russian legation. He had heard some rumour of it and went to the Russian, where he was assured that nothing could be more absurdly impossible.

'Of course, I don't want to spoil anything,' said the German, 'but I realize what a feather it would be for my cap if I could report it.'

'I know, I know; things are horribly dull, but this is positively grotesque. There is no truth in it whatever.'

'But you would tell me if it were true?'

'Certainly, my dear colleague.'

The German had hardly returned to his house before someone came rushing in to tell him that it was true and had happened. Back he went to the Russian, furious.

'Why did you lie to me?' he demanded. 'You did not need to tell me, but why lie?'

'Now, now,' soothed the Russian, 'why did you force me to lie to you?'

We did not know what was happening at home, and could not judge of the importance of what was happening in that far corner of the world.

We all lived within a hundred yards of our offices, so

lunched at home. The afternoons were generally more lively than the mornings, for Koreans came to pay court to the influential or to gather news for the palace. In return for the disclosures we made about each other's villainous designs, we angled for something upon which to base a dispatch for Washington. At five o'clock the juniors and most of the bachelor elders gathered at the club, for billiards, cocktails and our one card game, poker. Our poker games were continuous. In fact it was one long game, with interruptions; but it was innocuous as long as it remained among ourselves. We signed small notes for the amounts lost and once a month sent them through the clearing house. If one of us had notes that seemed too large, we held them back and waited till his winnings helped to balance, and cashed the little ones.

Once a newly arrived American engineer sat in and, not knowing our benign custom, cashed his chits. He built a neat bungalow and sent for a girl at home to come out and marry him; but we were cold about it and did not call on his wife for a long time. An artist who was passing through signed his losses with some rapid sketch and no name. He was disgusted when a Frenchman presented them for payment. He told me that even an unsigned sketch by him was worth more than any ordinary amount he might lose at poker. On another occasion I lost a friend, also a Frenchman. A new man was in our game and my friend was losing heavily and recklessly. I knew he happened to be hard up, so bought up his chits from the stranger. He got word that I was trying to corner his notes, and since every once in a while we were all suspicious of everybody he quarrelled violently about it and never spoke to me again.

From the club there was generally an official dinner or an informal one among ourselves. The official ones usually had Korean ministers of State. There was a good deal of music. None of the Europeans was very strict about office hours. Every one rode and riding parties were frequent. Picnics to the old palaces in the northern wards or expeditions to the fortress of Puk Han in the mountain peaks, or shooting parties to the river or the rice fields, kept us pretty well out of doors and active. Few of us ever took a holiday out of Korea. There were too many beautiful spots to explore where we were, in all directions, and every season to enjoy.

The seasons were marked more exactly than anywhere I have lived, each one just what it should be. The winters averaged thirteen degrees below, a clear, dry cold; the summers were hot with rain enough; the spring soft, and a mass of flowers; the autumn brilliant, clear sunshine and glorious moonlight.

Girls were at a premium. When any strayed in from the outside world, we acted for all the world like a crowd of cowboys, and became unbearable to each other until she had gone.

What we liked much better than the occasional girls who came were those occasions when we could make an excuse to call for a marine guard. Then, in the officers, we had new men to ride and shoot with, and we all took to training and boxing with the men, and to writing reports home to defend their reputations when some over-zealous spinster or clergyman objected to their brutal sports. Hutchison, head of the English language school, was always a godsend. He insisted on making an opposing soccer team for his Korean boys, and he was a magnificent cook. We played often and hard, generally captained by Arthur Turner, and then stayed to dinner, a marvellous banquet cooked by Hutchison himself, and lasting, with songs and music, far into the early morning.

The English were better off than anyone else, for they had someone over their young men who made them work a certain number of hours a day, either at Chinese or Korean, or reading things connected with their career. He was a sort of mentor to keep them steady and guide them generally. We do not have the same thing even now, for they do not make secretaries of legation overnight in the British service. They are students for years, and must work for promotion as they would under a tutor at Oxford. We are all officers from the start with no real authority over each other. If an American secretary ever learned anything in the old days it was by hard knocks and the experience of getting himself out of trouble unaided after he had got himself well in through sheer youthful arrogance and spirits.

CHAPTER VIII

THE ADVISER TO THE EMPEROR

IN 1899 I was invited to become adviser to the emperor, and to initiate him into the mysteries of European politics in their bearing on himself.

At the period of Japanese supremacy in Korea, after the defeat and final collapse of Chinese influence, a rule was forced on the emperor by which no foreign adviser might receive a salary larger than one hundred and fifty dollars a month. The purpose was clear enough. It was not intended that there should be an American successor to Judge Denny. A Japanese could live on that sum, and with a private salary or an expense account from his own government, he could live impressively. European advisers might be subsidized by their own governments, but the fact that they were would give a clear indication of their policy to Japanese observers, and that policy could be attacked in the Japanese press as partisan. No European or American of the right kind could be expected to live on such a salary, and a government subsidy was quite contrary to American practice. It was a move to break the American tradition and to eliminate the only real obstacle to annexation, for American influence was the only one which could not be attacked by Japanese politicians on the score of self-defence. There was no possible way of interpreting American influence in Korea as a menace to Japan or to anyone else. It was too obviously non-political and helpful to Korea.

It was quite clear that neither Japan nor Russia wanted a progressive Korea. Judge Denny, nevertheless, was followed by three Americans in the government who accepted that condition.

In 1899, Gen. Charles Legendre, adviser to the imperial household, died suddenly, and his death was followed by that of Clarence Greathouse. General Dye, military adviser and head of the military academy, retired and went home. Great pressure was brought to bear on the emperor by Russia, Japan, France, and Belgium, to replace them by distinguished nationals of theirs. The emperor turned to Mr Dinsmore, who had been American minister to Korea, but Dinsmore was in Congress and saw no attraction in giving up his constituency to return to Seoul.

Then a message came to me. I was enormously flattered, and at the very competent age of twenty-five, I felt capable of pulling the grand khan himself out of any amount of trouble, and I liked the Koreans. Our minister, Dr Horace Allen, approved, for he felt that if anything could be done for the salvation of the Koreans, only Americans could do it. I consulted John Hay, and his answer was prompt and emphatic:

'You will have a most interesting experience and you may and ought to derive from it something of considerable value to our government when, and *if*, you return. There is an 'if.' You have a very good chance not to return undamaged. You have only one complete certainty, and that is that the government of the United States will not, under any circumstances, be drawn into any complications which may arise out of your troubles. You do not represent the United States or American influence in any way. You are an adventurer, as far as we are concerned. When you have lived out your contract (if you do) it is logical to expect that the then Secretary of State will make use of a unique experience and take you back into the service.'

That was clear enough and satisfactory to me, though I did not realize that it killed any hope of pulling the

Koreans out of their troubles. What they wanted was not an individual American, but the goodwill of the American government, and through an American adviser they wanted the United States to act as a benevolent mediator for them with Europe and Japan.

In the welter of competition for spheres of influence and special interests neutrality could not possibly mean anything to the Oriental mind but weakness; in this case it might even mean to them disapproval of me on the part of my own government. Nor was it likely that any European diplomat would understand it. As adviser to the emperor I was either the instrument of the American minister's policies near the throne, or I represented nothing at all and was open prey to any other diplomat in the place. Protection of foreign officials in Asiatic governments by diplomacy ranging from official protest through naval demonstrations, to actual bombardment and landing expeditions had been drilled too deeply into backward countries for anyone to succeed as an independent and impartial adviser.

John Hay's instructions were meant to be taken literally by me and the legation, and they were. The legation washed its hands of me completely, as was necessary and proper under their orders from home. The very fact that I accepted, nevertheless, led both the Koreans and the diplomatic corps to believe at first that there must be some secret understanding with Hay, in spite of his official attitude. It was only gradually that the truth was driven home, as one legation after the other tried me out and our own remained passive as it was obliged to do. Under the first illusion I made a start. Then as opposition crystallized, the Koreans themselves gave up hope and lost interest, and finally decided to throw in their lot completely with the stronger of the two rivals: Russia or Japan.

I had a programme, and I had a party at court. Our objective was the neutralization of Korea in the event of conflict between Japan and Russia, in which America's interest while probably vague, would still be a real asset. In order to secure favourable attention for neutralization and absolute peace treaties between Korea and all the world, it was primarily necessary to work on two things: improvement in administration, and education. General education in Korea was non-existent. Under the old Chinese system there were requirements of scholarship to official appointment, and these were decided in annual competitive examination, which was all right in theory except that the examination was purely literary and classic, having nothing to do with modern conditions, and that selection opened the way wide to personal favour and bribery.

Even this method did not exist in Korea. There the appointing system had sunk to the lowest possible level. Appointment to office carried with it some degree of noble rank as well and so was sought for social reasons as well as for 'graft.' Administrative office was secured by nepotism and heavy payment, which, in turn, carried the necessity of recovering from the people the money expended to get it under the guise of taxation, and arbitrary taxation was the source of most of our internal disorders.

The bribery system of appointment was so complete that even the Japanese money lenders made a normal business of it. They would lend a candidate for some provincial post the necessary bribe money, at twelve per cent. a month (the usual rate also in land and crop transactions) to be repaid within a certain brief period of taking office. The first care of the new governor or district magistrate would be to raise whatever he had spent, plus interest, by taxation. Then he would need to raise the whole sum due from his district to the emperor by the same method, after which it was again necessary to tax the people in order to get as much as possible on his own account before being replaced by a new bidder for his post. The bribe money went to the emperor, and was not considered so immoral as it seems to us, for the land and the people belonged to him to dispose of as he wished. The sovereign was the State; all Korea and all Koreans were his, and all revenue was his, to be dispensed without control. His officials were simply his farmers-general. Probably because of these concepts of government Dumas' novels were the only foreign books which most educated Koreans grasped completely and read with understanding interest.

Any candidate was lucky who could get direct access to the emperor, for he got off cheaper than if he had to go through the whole palace hierarchy. Offices in the palace and around the imperial person were sought for that reason: they gave opportunity for patronage limited only by the energy and tact and guile of the incumbent.

Provincial administration was often rotten in that respect and in places it was frightful, for torture still existed ordinarily in the remoter back country, and was even revived occasionally in police procedure in the capital.

I knew all that, but I also knew that I had some influence with the emperor; he listened to me with confidence. I also knew that there was a considerable body of Korean officials who would prefer to be honest and were as decent as the system let them be. Several powerful nobles were heartily ashamed of the backwardness of their country and might be expected to help in a reform programme. I counted on the American party in the palace to become the chief advocates for reform, and on the American mission-trained natives and the oppressed peasants to support it enthusiastically. I believed that I could secure the co-operation of honest men like Sir John McLeavy Brown and Sir John Jordan, and that I could get the beginnings of an educational system out of unification of the various language schools, controlled by foreigners and supported by the Korean government, and could make all minor appointments from their graduates until we could develop further. Eventually I hoped to work out a definite tax system based upon a census, and to extend a definite code of procedure to the district and provincial courts. If I could get that far, and if I could show some measure of progress and reform, it seemed to me possible to hope for peace treaties and international agreements to guarantee our neutrality. I did not realize that it would take thirty years and a world war to bring people to the Kellogg treaties.

I had no intention to Americanize Korea. On the contrary, I wanted to keep the native culture as completely as possible, only familiarizing them with Western ways in sufficient degree to keep them out of unnecessary trouble. I wanted to keep foreign help to Korea international, but to make it co-operative rather than competitive. I did not see at first the hopelessness of trying to get English, Russian, French, German, and Japanese language schools out of the control of each legation and into co-operative effort for the benefit of the government that paid them; nor the impossibility of getting such a group, if formed, into co-operation with the schools of the American and French missionaries. It was much later that I realized how easy it was for those opposed to reform to make the peasants suspicious of a census as being a preliminary, not to uniform and simple taxation, but to increased taxation. There were plenty of opponents to reform. Everyone interested in plain and simple 'graft' as the basis of local government saw in my ideas destruction of their own chances and power. Governments interested in local disorders as a reason for intervention did not want reform.

Neither ought I to have expected to be able to unite the various foreign advisers of the Korean government into one body serving the interests of the country that supported them. They necessarily still thought of themselves as agents of their own legations.

Since the death of Legendre and Greathouse and the

retirement of Dye, a rigid French jurist had been brought in to reform Greathouse's legal reforms upon French colonial lines. A genial French adviser to the Postal Department was of necessity more broad in his views since he operated under the regulations of the international postal union, but had no power outside of his special service. A Danish adviser to the Telegraph Bureau in the Department of Communications played his lone hand in his own system. The French military advisers who succeeded Dye were naturally still part of the French army. Telephones and railways were operated under private concesssions, American and Japanese; a French railway line not yet constructed ran on paper to the Chinese border, and in all the public utility concessions Korea had a subsidy interest. All customs revenues remained under the control of McLeavy Brown.

My young efforts to get these foreign advisers and employees of the government to meet upon common ground and to agree upon some policy, no matter how simple and innocuous, were wrecked from the start with devastating completeness. As far as I know, not one legation, with the exception of the French, failed to protest to the emperor against my 'pernicious' activities. Collin de Plancy never intrigued and was personally always friendly and sympathetic.

Hope of neutralization and multilateral peace treaties faded out under the frank opposition of the Russian and Japanese ministers, Pavlow and Gonsuke Hayashi, who found for the first and only time something that they could see alike. All hope of reform succumbed to the hostility of those who because of their national interests did not want it, since disorder was the excuse for intervention. My next four years were occupied fully with attempts to meet individual abuses rather than a general condition, to prevent or hold down local disorders, to prevent foreign stimulation of disorders and to do what little any individual might do to keep the peace, and to

hold off as long as possible the collapse of the harassed
kingdom.

The initial difficulty was that of the low pay fixed for
advisers by the rule imposed years before by the
Japanese. The solution was disconcertingly simple. The
word for adviser used in the agreement was *Komungwan*. I
was therefore called *Chanigwan* which meant the same
thing. By calling me another name the Koreans felt that
they were freeing themselves from an imposed rule and
were free to pay me what they pleased – which turned out
to be literally true when the hard-bitten old, miner Ye
Yong Ik got control of the imperial purse. In my contract
it was provided that no other adviser could be engagd
without my consent and that if engaged he must co-
operate with me.

I was given a house near the legation quarters and
rooms inside the palace, with a staff of interpreters with
some knowledge of the principal foreign languages,
several writers and a Chinese scholar to put memorials
into the classic writing of the court. My chief interpreter
and principal intermediary with the emperor was Hyen
Sang Kien, a young noble, very smart in appearance and
dress, with a fluent though not perfect knowledge of
French. His chief asset outside of his pleasant personality
was that he really knew always what I was talking about,
though he had never travelled either at home or abroad;
nothing was foreign to him. The second was a delightful
young man of a noble family going back into pre-history,
Ko Hei Kiung. Ko, who had also never travelled, knew
English so perfectly and was so naturally at home in the
customs of good society anywhere that when I sent him to
England later as secretary of a special mission, several of
the most conservative people at the English court took
him down to stay in their homes. He was a perfect example
of the Korean proverb that 'a gentleman is known though
he be naked in the desert.' Hyen was extremely ambitious,
which in the end was his undoing. Ko was conservative,

scrupulously honest and absolutely reliable. My Japanese interpreter was 'Black' Hyen, a cousin of the first – an older man, taciturn, with a heavy pirate beard which gave him his nickname. I never could make him out. The two seniors were the heads of my office. I used them for confidential work and for personal audiences with the emperor or conversations with nobles or officials who spoke no language but their own. The others I used as translators.

The method of preparing a memorial to secure exact translation of what I wanted to say involved a great deal of work. First I wrote it all out. Then I got Ko to translate it into Korean. I would then get Hyen to retranslate it to me verbally in French, or one of the others to read it to me in some other language, to be sure the full sense had been preserved. Once sure of that I had it set up in the ceremonial court language, so complicated and archaic that it is sure to lose the sense of anything unknown in the time of Abraham. That being done, I had it read to me again in a foreign language by one of the men who had not seen it before. Finally the principal writer was called in, for a communication to the emperor or to any person of rank must be set up in writing as perfect as an artist's work for the salon. One more reading back to me and I was ready to go to the emperor, tell him through Hyen or Ko what I had to say and leave the document with him to read over at his leisure, which I am sure he never did. Even with all these precautions one could not be absolutely sure of getting a message straight. In the case of a number of conspirators who had given endless trouble for years but had been brought back from Japan on a promise of amnesty, I was consulted on the subject of attainder. I explained the mediaeval theory of the effects of high treason and its punishment even in the families and heirs of the person attainted, and added carefully that it was a custom we in the West no longer believed in or practised and that in any case these men were protected by the emperor's amnesty. I found, however, that my paper had been changed in transit and that I had been made to say exactly the opposite. The men were strangled in prison, and as they had been promised the protection of the Japanese government, besides the imperial amnesty, it made a very awkward incident with the Japanese, and was vigorously exploited by the Japanese press. Unfortunately it went quite far to justify their contention that the Korean government could not be trusted.

In addition to my staff there were several men in the palace who were real friends. Min Yong Whan, Min Sang Ho and their cousin Prince Min Yong Ki all members of the late queen's clan, had the interests of Korea very much at heart. The two former had lived abroad; all three were powerful nobles at home. Min Sang Ho was the most perfect type of Korean aristocrat one could choose; his delicately aquiline features have been preserved by Hubert Vos in his collection of portraits of Korea, China, and India. Min Yong Whan killed himself when all attempt at internal reform failed and the Japanese took his country. He is honoured by Koreans as a great patriot and martyr. I never knew to what Prince Min Yong Ki was comparable until recent years, when Arthur Waley published the 'Lady Murasaki's Chronicle of Genji,' the 'Shining One' of Japan's troubadour days. All three of these men had access to the palace when they pleased.

A friend, though not at all of the nobility, was Kang Sok Ko, the chief eunuch, a powerful personage. Outside of the palace was the jovial Governor Ye, who ruled the capital. He had lived in Washington and was devoted to everything American. He was a shrewd and kindly man, ambitious but cautious. Toward the end, just before the débâcle, he sent for me suddenly in the middle of the night. I found him fearfully swollen and hardly able to speak, but still gay and laughing. I offered to send at once for a foreign doctor.

'Why!' he said, 'you people don't understand these

things. I am dying, and besides my old mother has no confidence in foreigners. I sent for you for two things: you must promise to save my son and what property you can for him – and I want you to send immediately and find out how the other men are who dined with me to-night.'

He would not tell me who his host had been.

'You can find that out for yourself if you want. You can't do anything about it.'

My messenger came back to say that only one of the guests had survived; the others were dead, with the same symptoms as the governor.

'Yes' – he chuckled, 'I ought to have known better, an old bird like me. It doesn't matter. We can't save the country. Save my son for old friendship's sake, for I have really been your friend.' And he smiled at me and died. A few years ago his son, mature and prosperous, wrote me to remind me of that old friendship.

Another member of the circle was Ye Hak Kiun, General Dye's assistant and now head of the military academy. He too was a good friend. When the Russo-Japanese war came he escaped to Shanghai with Hyen Sank Kien, took to opium and died in poverty.

At the head of the foreign office was another man, a very able one, Pak Chai Soon. In spite of the fact that a minister of state in Korea was simply a tool for court intrigue and was never a responsible official, he filled his office with dignity and discretion.

While I was in charge of the legation, I had a bout with him, though it did not lessen our friendship.

The emperor had promised Allen to open Peng Yang to foreign residence. Peng Yang, the northern city, in the province of the same name, was intensely conservative. Powerful people there urged the emperor to revoke his promise and as the province was intensely loyal and the recruiting ground of his best fighting troops he gave in, and when the edict was published it was not the city that was opened but a small place in the province unsuitable for foreign trade and residence. Pak upheld the wording of the edict. I insisted on the emperor's promise and won. Moreover, Peng Yang had the reputation of being one of the four wickedest cities of ancient and modern history and I was determined to let in the sun and fresh air. That incident has been recently cited as a typical case of American imperialistic aggression. The author of the essay on the subject could not possibly know that Pak agreed with me, but had to obey his instructions.

Unquestionably anyone a day over twenty-five, knowing Korea as I did, would never have attempted to stop a war between Russia and Japan single-handed. Looking back at it now, I rather like the gesture. I went into it with my eyes as wide open as they could be at the time, though certainly I could not see where it was all leading, and I doubt that anybody else could. I went into it because I was sorry for the helpless emperor and felt vigorous enough to help him, and believed really that since co-operation had never been tried it ought to be possible to enlist the help of the diplomats at Seoul in an honest programme of reform. I also remembered Rockhill's advice to watch and learn, and I was watching the manoeuvres of the great ones in the capitals of the world work out through the little men on the battle line. John Hay was perfectly right. I would learn through trial and error much that could be of great value later to our own government, if I survived the experiment. So was Secretary Root, years later, when he told me that I could never be a diplomat if I tried with both hands, according to the Department's concept of a diplomat; for I had learned to do things on my own judgment and to fight my own way through all obstacles and guard my own head, which does not make a good secretary.

All true, but I would not have given it up for anything; I was determined to see it through.

CHAPTER IX

LIFE AT COURT AND NATIVE SPORTS

M Y nights were supposed to be passed in the palace, my days on His Majesty's business; so I had to have quarters in town as well as near the emperor.

An American missionary had built a house overlooking a very sacred spot. Once in a while some foreigner would do that, in spite of the violation it involved, both of native etiquette and of actual law. The Korean authorities never dared apply the law to a foreigner, for it involved confiscation of the property to the Crown and heavy penalties, which no self-respecting legation would allow. The only remedy was purchase by the emperor for as much as the foreigner dared ask, and as his claim was generally supported by his legation, he dared greatly.

In this case, the quite ugly house, built of brick in the mid-Victorian style of the Middle West, was bought at an exorbitant price and given me to use. By the time I left Korea it was comfortable enough for the Japanese to take it over as their general staff headquarters. To me its attraction lay in the park I planted round it, into which I turned all the fawns and bear cubs, young cranes, goldfish, and other helpless things brought me from the country. They all prospered and lived quite happily together and increased more or less like guinea-pigs, to the discomfort of those who objected to being chased by ambitious young bucks and who did not like bears. A bear is a one-master animal. Mine obeyed me but were not nice with other people. Since there were some misguided people in town who did not like me, I did not encourage my bears to be polite to strangers.

This house was used more for official entertainment by the palace people than as my home, which sometimes led to amusing encounters. I returned one evening late from a hard journey in the interior, dirty, unshaven, muddy, and exhausted. I came in through the servant quarters, to find the house lighted from floor to roof and a great bustle of palace cooks. It annoyed me, and I threw open the pantry door to the dining-room to see what was going on in my absence. All the dignitaries of the court were seated around my table, and in the place of honour stood a quite obvious American making a speech about the coming World's Fair. He broke off, stared at me and asked me what I wanted.

'A bath, a shave and food, thanks very much.'

'You can't get that here, my man, this is a private house.'

'Quite so,' I answered. 'It is a private house. It is mine. Would you mind telling me what you are doing in it?'

'Oh, I beg your pardon! I am the commissioner general of the World's Fair. My name is John Barrett' – which was my first meeting with my very good friend, whom I later succeeded in the legation at Panama and who created that masterpiece, the Pan-American Union from an obscure bureau of Latin-American affairs.

My headquarters were in the palace. To the great joy and unceasing ribald comment of every young diplomatic colleague I was given there the fourth side of the building which housed the palace ladies on two, and the eunuchs on the third side of a quadrangle.

Under an old custom which had grown up out of palace revolutions, the emperor did not sleep at night. The great palace gates closed firmly at sundown and a small postern gate opened only by his personal order, under supervision of one of his most trusted attendants, to let in or out some one person at a time. All ministers of State, nobles paying ceremonial call or other natives entitled to audience came in before sunset and waited, sometimes until the gates were opened again at sunrise. Night was the time for the transaction of State affairs, unless these clashed with more serious things like a poetical contest, the choice of silks or perfumes for the wardrobe or the trying out of a new dancer.

All imperial business, such as ministers' daily reports, policy to be made, meetings of the great council, were interspersed with, and more often than not supersded by, His Majesty's *menus plaisirs*. It was Alexandre Dumas in oriental setting.

I was expected to be on duty from sundown to sunrise, ready at any time for an audience or to answer a question or give advice on some report.

Sooner or later all official business came my way. If the emperor himself did not send to ask my opinion, some one of the eunuchs was sure to hurry in to give me what he had heard from behind a screen, as he understood it, in order to have a ready-made opinion to throw into debate and mark up a credit for his knowledge.

These curious eunuch people wandered in and out of my quarters at all times, questioning about everything, restless, eternally dissatisfied and greedy. Under no other conditions could one possibly gain so complete an insight into the secret workings of palace diplomacy in the East as by living among them. Although they were probably the most influential people at the Korean court, because of their access to the emperor at any time, their influence was always harmful. They were generally taken from poor families, had no education whatever, native or foreign, and were generally quite illiterate. They were warped and suspicious by nature, jealous, moody, and prone to sudden anger and vindictive hatred. Their one all-absorbing passion was money, and any way to get it was legitimate. Contrary to the usual belief, they were all married. Prosperous eunuchs adopt very young eunuch boys to bring up as their sons, so that there are eunuch families hoping to succeed to a fortunate father eunuch.

They are not quite like the traditional eunuch of the Near East. In Korea their primary function was personal attendance on the emperor. They were theoretically supposed to stand apart from all worldly interests and passions; in theory they were austere and ascetic persons unsullied by the world. Only such a person was fit to approach the sacred perosn of the monarch familiarly. Practically they were all the contrary of any such ideal, but it was convenient to be blind to that for the sake of the theory, although if they ever gave rise to public scandal their punishment was terrific.

Because of the convention concerning their theoretical spiritual qualities, they had come to represent a sort of priesthood. Sacrifice to Heaven, that is to the Supreme Being, was reserved to the emperor in person. It might be delegated, however, and generally was delegated, to a eunuch as being nearest to the emperor. On the same theory they were made guardians of the royal tombs and sacrificial temples, and were put in charge of the conduct of the palace ladies.

These ladies were the wives and minor consorts of royalty and their attendants. Probably only the wives of the eunuchs themselves led a more miserable existence than these unfortunates. Women of the people and women servants of the palace could come and go as they pleased, day or night. Women of the better class and of the nobility could visit each other at night, strongly guarded as they passed through the streets. The public dancers and singing girls without whom no Korean entertainment was complete were as free as the air, and formed the only approach to native feminine society there was. They at least had some semblance of culture and education as part of their preparation for public entertaining. The poor palace ladies, however, were barred completely from all worldly contamination. Members of the harem were supposed to live the lives of contemplative nuns. The slightest curiosity about outside affairs,

the slightest communication with them entailed the
severest punishment for everybody concerned. One of
the eunuchs, nevertheless, at the risk of his life and hers,
constantly brought me requests from the crown princess
who lived next door, for Western reading. I never saw
her, nor discussed her with anyone, but I was impressed
by her mind. I sent her all the translations I could find in
Chinese or Japanese of Western books of history, science,
geography, philosophy and art, and European novels. A
good deal of it was intelligible to her. When she found a
difficulty, her intermediary would come and sit with me
and discuss it. Her comments and questions were
remarkably shrewd. I suspect that the emperor knew all
about it, for there is no secret possible for long in an
Oriental court. Perhaps he remembered that his own
poor queen had been hungry for Western knowledge,
and was satisfied to let his son's wife have it too.

A remarkable person who used to sit with me night
after night was the emperor's private historian, and teller
of tales. There is a curious likeness, and much more than
a likeness at times, between these tales and Sir Richard
Burton's collections from the Arabic and Persian. Japanese
and Chinese tales have a character of their own; they are
plainly indigenous. Many of the Korean tales are identical
with those of Bagdad or North Africa, and might be tex-
tual translations. They are told with such a wealth of
gesture, mimicry, and intonation that they are often perfectly intelligible even to one having little knowledge of
the language. While more than broad, they are not
necessarily coarse, and can be uproariously funny. The
art of telling in Korea consisted in saying anything at all
without offending against the fastidiousness of aristo-
cratic etiquette by blatant vulgarity and coarseness.
Much had to be left unsaid but conveyed in such a manner
as to provoke a laugh from nobles to whom easy laughter
was unseemly. That same art of leaving things unsaid and
of tricking people into self-betrayal was practised in

another way, in conversation between two nobles, strangers, who might chance to meet. Each grade in Korean society is indicated by the verbal forms used in conversation. You change your verbal endings according to the social position of the person with whom you are speaking, and it is very important to give exactly the right shade. If you miss it, either for a degree too high or a degree too low, you brand yourself as being unused to court life, a rustic and not a man of the world.

Two men meeting by chance, unknown to each other even by name, but apparently belonging to the noble class, would spar for hours in conversation, never ending a verb, each trying to conceal his own rank and place the other's exactly, by every possible device. They would develop a kind of neutral language until one would triumphantly guess the precise status and social antecedents of his adversary partner in the game and use the corresponding verbal form. If he were wrong the other would at once use a form of verbal ending obviously lower than the guesser's rank, to indicate that had he been quite a gentleman he could not have made such a social blunder.

Part of the polite science of conversation was poetry. As in Japan in the ninth century, gentlemen might discuss any person or any subject in witty and impromptu verse or in anagrams. In all these social games little mannerisms like an intonation, the handling of a fan, the use of perfume or the manner of toying with some ornament of one's costume, distinguished the new man from the perfect courtier, to those who knew the rules.

Among intimate friends, classic poetry fixed some special private name, unknown outside of the select circle. Foreign names are difficult to pronounce in any Oriental country. They are particularly hard to write in the Chinese characters which are the universal means of communication among the educated men of the Far East, even when they cannot speak each other's language.

When I came to Japan, my own name, Sands, was impossible to pronounce or to write. It might have gone as
San-dzu, but that does not mean anything, and a name
must have a meaning so that it can be written. So my
name became *San-Do* in Japan, to fit the Chinese characters *Shan* (mountain) and *Tao* (island) which has the advantage of being also a well-known and well-born name,
pronounced *Yama-shima* in Japanese. My Japanese intimates
always called me by that name.

In Korea, where the Chinese classics were better
known than in Japan, it was recalled that there is a famous
Chinese poem concerning the strength of the mountain
and the depth of the sea which conveyed to the wits and
scholars a friendly allusion to my own position, by analogy
to the isolation of some rocky island beaten by the waves,
and so two words from the poem became my private
name in the inner circle of my friends, and was cut on a
seal with which all my private correspondence with them
was signed.

In the spring and autumn when people were tempted
abroad by the new flowers or the moon, poetry parties
were the fashion. Groups of courtiers young or old, selected a notably beautiful spot, borrowed or hired a house
generally on the river, and spent the days fishing and the
nights in poetical composition and criticism. With
experts in this art, all conversation had to be in appropriate verse and in a form agreed upon in advance. It was
not easy to keep up all day no matter what one was doing,
but the slightest slip was punished by a fine, generally a
present of wine from the victim to the one who caught
him up with a better verse.

Among Korean gentlemen drinking was not heavy.
There was a good deal of drunkenness among the lower
people though not nearly as much drinking as among
people of northern Europe or in America, for in general
they could not stand much. They were all heavy smokers,
which habit American missionaries dutifully tried to

curb, and enormous eaters, but a very little drink was enough to unbalance them, as is true generally of Japanese, though I found notable exceptions.

Fishing was a sport recognized among gentlemen. Shooting with guns was not, nor riding. Both were permitted, however, to men who bore a military title, under the new dispensation. Few of the bearers of high military rank were trained men. We had only the first beginnings of a corps of officers, graduates of the military academy. The director of the academy, Gen. Ye Hak Kiun had absorbed from General Dye some idea of how to run a cadet school. He had sent some of the graduates to Japan for advanced training, and they had done very well, but fell promptly under suspicion of being secret Japanese agents when they returned to Korea, and were not used in the regiments. I did what I could to relieve their position. I rode with them and shot with them and even built them a clubhouse in a corner of my gardens, where they could meet and live as long as they liked, and kept a Chinese servant there to look after them. Nothing could have been better calculated to put them against the government than this policy of suspicion. By keeping them with me I hoped to counteract it.

Early one morning at breakfast, after my return from the palace, two of them came in to see me, deadly green in the face with deep black lines under the eyes, to tell me they had spent the night at my club. I was curious to know how they had spent the night. They had sent out for a bottle of something, they said, to pass the time. One bottle of anything seemed too little to have wrecked two rather sturdy lieutenants so completely, so I sent for the empty bottle. It was absinthe which they had drink in liqueur glasses without water. I still do not think it was possible, but they did it and survived.

For our shooting parties we went well outside of the city to some royal tomb, though small game abounded everywhere. All royal tombs, no matter how ancient,

were supposed to be surrounded by a decorous silence,
and lying in some sheltered valley were closed in by
forest. Near them in a clearing is the house of the resident
guardian, and often a Buddhist monastery with a few
mendicant monks. The outside slopes of the surrounding
hills are stripped bare of trees, so that these places
become the day refuge of wolves, bears, leopards, and
tigers as they pass along the mountain ridges from one
end of the peninsula to the other, and there were always
deer. I was given the special privilege of getting rid of
them, and whenever I was notified, I rode out sometimes
alone, sometimes with foreigners but more often with
Gen. Ye Hak Kiun and some of the officers who had been
trained to rifles.

At one lovely spot, Kwang-neung, about twenty miles
from Seoul, I had six native hunters. These men are
pariahs in Korean society, as are butchers, tanners and
grave diggers, or others who handle dead things. Koreans
may not associate with them directly in any way. While
very strict about that rule in town, General Ye and his
companions did exactly as I did about it when we were
with them. The hunters were the experts, trackers and
guides quite as good as any Indian, and in the woods we
put ourselves in their hands, just as one would in the
Maine woods. They were interesting people, these pariah
hunters. All were well over six feet tall. One of them was
florid in complexion with red hair, red bushy beard, and
bright blue eyes. They could walk for ever, without food,
and were excellent woodsmen, and good shots with their
antiquated matchlocks. They would laugh at us for miss-
ing a fine shot with our Winchester carbines, when they
could hit as far as their iron tubes would carry. Their
matchlocks were loaded with hand-mixed coarse black
powder and iron pellets, hammered into something near
a round shape. On the pan they scattered a finer powder
which was touched off with the burning end of a long
string wound around the right arm. Ammunition was

precious, and their angular bullets carried neither far nor with great force, so a hunter had to walk up on a tiger or bear and shoot him from a few feet away to get him. The leader of my hunters was a Presbyterian, 'because the Christian missionaries can associate with outcasts, and I feel like a man in a Christian church.' There was no lack of manhood in these fellows. The simple Korean country-man was capable of great development.

A very noble but exceedingly expensive sport was hawking. I kept hawks for a while, for the experience and as an attraction to the young courtiers, but it was too troublesome to go on with.

The hawks were large like our chicken hawk. Two expert falconers, heavily paid, and a dog man to follow with the retriever, were necessary for each bird.

The hawk was taken out, just as in older Europe or in Central Asia to-day, perched on a heavy gauntlet and hooded, with a small silver bell on his collar to locate him after flight. He is not trained to return to the hawker's wrist, but to the dog. The dog is of no particular breed, and is rarely broken to retrieve. His duty is to find the fallen game and guard it until it is picked up. The hawk is trained to go and perch on his back until the hunters come up with him, and they follow on foot. The broken hill country is not suited to hawking from horseback. It is a delightful sport. Pheasants are the easiest game. They are plentiful and fly straight away for the far side of the narrow valleys, the hawk a little above until he can strike at the neck or head, and he rarely strikes until just before the pheasant reaches safety on the other side. The stout, elderly noble waits in full sight of the chase and joins it at his leisure while younger blood runs at top speed with the hawkers and miscellaneous beaters and follows behind the two birds.

Bustards and ducks give the same sort of straightaway run. Hares double and throw the hawk off and may get clear away. Cranes are the kings of hawking. They try to

rise above their pursuer, and are as tireless in flight as he
is. Their long lance bills are always ready to impale him
when he strikes, and they fight with their heads. The
hawk is kept fierce by starving and teasing. That is why
two men are needed for each bird. He must be fed only
enough to keep his strength and never enough to satisfy
him. He may not be allowed to sleep before the chase
more than just enough to avoid weakness. One man is
constantly awake to tease the bird into wakefulness.
Then too, he is subject to innumerable ailments, according to hawkers' craft, and if one pursues this noble game,
it is etiquette to believe absolutely and without comment
all that the hawker tells you on that score, and to pay him
what he asks for rare medicines and remedies, equally
without comment.

Archery was still a live sport and almost more than a
sport, for it was not long since that bows had been used in
war. The bows were shorter than the American or the old
English bows, but much heavier and broader. They were
made of wide strips of ox horn cunningly welded together
and were more powerful than the former. I could not
even bend one, though the Koreans who practised constantly could send their yard-long reed shafts tipped with
iron very accurately and with incredible rapidity and
strength. They never hesitated to take one on in target
competition against a .45 Colt revolver at a hundred
yards. I have seen them make a series of bull's-eyes at two
hundred and even make a target at three hundred
yards.

I was well stocked with horses, as a necessity rather
than a luxury, for travel in the interior was dependent
upon horse or palankeen. General Voyron, the French
commander in chief in China, sent four Arab stallions to
the emperor which were turned over to my use. They
were the best travelling horses I ever knew, even though,
as I learned later, they had all been culled out of the
chasseurs d'Afrique for incurable vices. I had taken their

little wickednesses for granted as belonging to the character of Arab horses, not realizing that what a chasseur d'Afrique cannot ride cannot be ridden. Strangely enough, though difficult to ride, none of them ever but once played any of the tricks on me for which they had been banished from the French army.

In order to know the country I was trying to help, I had to get out in every direction as often as possible. I had to go quickly to any place where I heard of trouble that might be made a pretext for foreign intervention. Just as I had to learn to know the nobles by living intimately with them and sharing their unofficial lives, so I had to know the lower people in the provinces by going out unknown and without a suite, and living with them whenever I could. I had several faithful servants whom I could trust absolutely on these occasions; one who had been a soldier, one a good Korean groom who had been brought up by Japanese and could pass for one, and one a high-wayman and murderer who had been given me by Governor Ye.

The governor asked me one day if I needed a man who was so fearless and such a good shot that it seemed a pity to execute him.

'He is a famous bandit,' he said, 'and our soldiers caught him asleep. He is to be tried for murder, and I shall have to have him strangled. If you want him, I shan't try him. I can tell him you have interceded for him and that he must serve you faithfully or be hanged.'

I did need a person like that, if he could be trusted, so agreed to try him out.

I was going on a shooting expedition a few days later and when I got to Kwang-neung, missed my watch, a precious heirloom. I sent one of my men back to look for it. He reported that he had not found it, and knowing all the other people in the household, it occurred to him that the new man must have had access to the house, in spite of being forbidden to come in. Sure enough, I had called him in myself, being a powerful fellow, to help move some furniture the day before I left. My man then found out where the ex-bandit's wife lived, and asked her for the 'pawn ticket.' She denied having one at first, but when he told her that it meant her husband's death if there was no pawn ticket she produced one, and a few pointed remarks to the pawnbroker produced the watch. The thief was with me when the watch was brought back. I handed it to him to keep preciously for me, and to learn to know it, so that it could never be lost again. He looked steadily at me, smiled a little dark smile and prostrated himself in the universal Oriental genuflexion.

'*Tai-in!*' was all he said: 'Master!'

I never had the slightest trouble with him again.

People called the Koreans the greatest cowards on earth, and I suppose they were in a sense, for, oppressed by everybody at home and abroad for centuries, they cringed before authority. That is, they cringed until things became unbearable and something broke, and then, like the Russian peasant when he goes wild, they destroyed blindly and completely. I cannot believe, though, that a man is a coward who will walk up on a tiger and kill him at arm's length with a very inadequate matchlock gun, or a blow with an iron mace. The same man would cringe abjectly to someone in authority immediately afterward, but that is something else. The Korean soldiers at Kang Wha fort stood against the American navy with their matchlocks and jingals, until American rifles set fire to their wadded clothes, and died where they stood. The sailors did not think them cowards. Neither did the French whose landing party was driven off at the same island fort. They were clumsy fighters and their weapons archaic, but there was the making of a good man in the Korean peasant. He was worth saving. The more I saw of him the more I determined to stand by him and see what one man could do about it.

CHAPTER X

OFTEN the whole night would go by without consultation on State business, though the emperor never failed in the early days to send a messenger several times to ask if I were well. On those nights all the idle courtiers in the palace would come and sit with me and gossip intimately, since we were all in the palace together and, therefore, above the ordinary formalities of outside life.

One of the constant visitors to my rooms on these occasions was a venerable old gentleman with a long silky white beard who had held an office years before corresponding more or less to a combination of commissioner of police, state prosecutor, and trial judge all in one. He was fully of memories of the early contacts with foreigners from the 'body snatching' incident and the massacre of the *General Sherman* crew to the persecution of Catholics in 1866.

The first was a piratical voyage from China to rob royal tombs, on the supposition that ancient Korean kings were buried in golden coffins with great treasures. According to the tale a French priest had attached himself to the expedition in order to get into the country after missionaries were barred. Some say that he instigated the voyage, and worked on the cupidity of loose characters about the port to get them to set him over. My Korean friend knew only that attempts had been made to rifle the sacred graves by people who were forbidden to enter the country and heard that among them was a Christian priest to whom entrance was particularly forbidden.

He supposed that the voyage of the *General Sherman* was another such attempt, and he had taken what he thought was a patriotic part in the massacre of the crew. Korea had been so ravaged for hundreds of years by the Chinese and Japanese that there was nothing strange in the Koreans' fear of foreigners and their determination not to admit them. They looked on these expeditions as piratical and attacked them, and when two naval punitive expeditions turned up at Kang Wha, sent by alleged governments they had never heard of, they began to believe that all Western foreigners were pirates. The old gentleman confirmed the tale current in Seoul among the natives about the last massacre of Christians.

Tai Won Kun, that vigorous personality who attempted to found a dynasty through his young son and the tragic Min princess, appears to have been highly superstitious. Having consulted his favourite soothsayer on the permanency of his dynasty he was told that this would depend on the death of . . . (the fortune teller used a word which is translatable by 'ten thousand'). The regent, it seems, was aghast at such a holocaust of his subjects, but believing that a formidable blood sacrifice was demanded of him to placate hostile spirits, hit upon the happy expedient of sacrificing ten thousand Christians, who never would be missed and, moreover, had dealings with foreigners. Hence the terrific persecution of 1866. Before he tallied the required number, however, his seer told him that it was not ten thousand men in general whose death was needed, but a person unfriendly to him whose intimate nickname could be so translated, and the persecution stopped.

My old friend, who was in office during that time, told me that he had great difficulty in accustoming himself to violent death. Torture made him ill, but as a matter of duty he sat in the torture cells day after day, half fainting with horror. Finally, he attempted to steel himself by having his meals brought there during the martyrdom of the

Christians, and one day felt that he had triumphed in the cause of duty, when a portion of some mangled body flew across the room and lit on his meal table – and by a supreme effort of will, he removed it with his chopsticks and, somewhat hastily, finished his repast.

There was no animosity in the old man to foreigners or to Christians. He admitted that Koreans had all been mistaken and regretted it, and he never omitted to thank Heaven that torture had been abolished at least officially by foreign influence.

Torture had been abolished by law it is true, but it was too deeply part of native custom to root out easily. The practice is so widespread in the Far East that the French were obliged to admit it into their colonial legal code, though in a mild form, to be sure. They found out that in their war on river pirates, they could not find witnesses and could not expect to, for it was certain death for a villager to tell on his neighbour. Confession by a witness under torture was admitted, however, in village custom. If a witness returning from court could show marks of torture on his body, he was safe. The French, therefore, paddled every witness thoroughly in a piracy case, with the full consent of the paddled, before ever a question was asked of him. They beat him with an instrument rather like a canoe paddle or a thin cricket bat, on a part where he could not be injured, but where bruises would show up beautifully. After that he could tell the truth, if he were capable of that, without fear of death from his fellow villagers. The bruises had to show though when he got home. Koreans practised that minor form of torture also, sometimes on witnesses and sometimes as a punishment for light offences. Much more serious was the boot, the same thing we all used in the Middle Ages. Two blocks of wood were fastened securely together on the outside of the victim's legs, so that they would not yield. Wedges were then driven between corresponding blocks on the inside of both legs with heavy mallets, so that gradually the leg bones were crushed. This was used principally to extort confessions, as it was in fair Europe. Another form, just as painful, consisted in lashing both legs together tightly at ankle and knee. Two staves were then inserted between the shinbones and pulled like levers in opposite directions by powerful coolies; this threw all the joints out beyond cure. No one who had been through either torture ever expected to walk again. There were also various pressures on delicate parts of the body easy to injure permanently, and red-hot cutting pincers that would nip a piece out of the body or lop off a finger or toe. Then there were the weight tortures: the piling of increasing weights on a person's body until he confessed or died, the *peine forte et dure* of mediaeval Europe. Execution was done by strangling. A light cord loop was passed around the neck, and a stout stick passed through it, and given to some able-bodied person to twist until no longer necessary. Under the vigilance of American missionaries in the interior and French priests or Japanese merchants, the worst of these practices were dying out. The trouble with it was that provincial governors and magistrates had been given no code of law and court practice to supplant the old Oriental idea of the wise though despotic judge with full power to detect and punish misbehaviour. Those magistrates who ceased to use their only power became helpless to keep order, while those who tortured were generally doing it to extort money. Once in a while a magistrate would throw himself on your mercy, and ask how in the world he was to govern except by methods the people knew.

None of these Korean lapses from a new ideal were as bad as the corresponding forms of official cruelty in China. I remember being unable once to get my passport visaed in Peking because the whole of that legation world I needed to see had gone with cameras to a crucifixion and slicing. Parricide and the murder of a husband were punished that way. I did not go, but the French postmaster in Tientsin showed me the photographs he had made, which it is perhaps not necessary to describe. The crucifixion was real, and the knife used in slicing the living body was blunt toward the end of the process. I did not like the collection.

Those practices we did not have, and whether the Chinese needed to be ruled that way or not, Koreans did not need to be, for our people were peaceful and harmless unless driven to desperation by abuse. There never were people more easily governed. I was determined to stamp out those tortures that still existed while the French colonial jurist was reforming Clarence Greathouse' reforms, and wherever I heard of them there I appeared swiftly and administered the same sort of despotic justice myself to the official culprit— without torture. There was one hard-bitten old miscreant who refused to come up to Seoul to explain charges of that kind against him, or to receive me if I went down country to him, and was rather truculent about it. I decided to take him by surprise and the last night of the journey rode hard with an imposing retinue to catch him as soon as his gates opened at sunrise, before he was aware of me. Once inside, I proposed to be very fierce with him indeed, and to take advantage of the loss to his dignity if he had to come out before he had time to dress.

One of my men who knew the country told me that the great gate and the front wall were about all that could stop me; that there was no back wall and that I could ride straight in from behind, through the orchard and private garden. I decided to do that, and the tables were turned against me most completely. I suddenly found myself face to face with the old man, in the very first stages of his early morning toilet, and in such a situation that it was I who was embarrassed, and had to ride through pretending not to see him. It turned out all right, for he was too terrified at the sight of my armed riders to take advantage of my barbarous breach of etiquette. I was forced to wait

for him, which gave him the edge, but we reached an
accord and he promised to be good. They generally did
out in the country when one had a chance to explain what
one wanted for Korea and why. It was the city grafters, as
always and everywhere, who were hard to handle.

On these swift rides through the country I generally
travelled light – a light stable boy riding a second horse
and leading a third, my equipment distributed in
saddlebags on all three. Most Koreans cannot ride, so
when speed was necessary I would take a young cavalry
instructor along from the military academy as interpreter. Often I would go out with only the groom, and
often too quite alone, to see things I could not find
officially. On one of these latter lonely journeyings I
learned why Englishmen dress for dinner, no matter
where they are. I had been riding for days on bypaths,
living on the country, sleeping in vermin-infested huts,
and one night in a halting place for pack-drivers where,
unknown to me until the morning, a leper shared my
blanket. I was unshaven and dirty and feeling rather hard
and superior to civilization. Late in the afternoon I came
out of the hills on to a travelled road and fell in with a
young Englishman, exploring. He had a caravan of laden
ponies with him, his cook and an English servant. He
took me civilly enough, and asked me to dine with him.
Toward sunset he made camp. His man put up a screen,
unfolded a rubber tub into which the cook poured hot
water, and while his master shaved and bathed, he laid a
table with white things, and glass and silver. Presently we
sat down to an excellent meal, he dressed and I filthy. It
struck me then that one reason why Englishmen turn out
such good administrators in backward countries is that
they do not try to maintain superiority to the native by
force but by keeping themselves up to the mark. I have
seen it so often since, in the tropics. The minute a man
who is living alone in the jungle lets himself go in the little
things, he begins to slip in the big ones. Ever since that

evening I have looked upon the dinner coat in the middle of the desert or the monocle in a firing trench with respect and understanding.

These lonely rides were never dangerous, though they were supposed to be. Most of the mountain folk were quite unused to foreigners, and very curious about everything. They were kindly and hospitable and crowded one's night quarters to suffocation, if not frightened by harsh behaviour. Whether of high degree or low they are easily frightened by violence. There is a typical story of that, concerning two village merchants who loaded their goods on a pony and drove it over a high mountain pass to the town. Halfway up the hill on the way back two robbers sprang out at them, not armed, but shouting that they were robbers. The two villagers ran leaving everything behind, and the robbers drove the pony up the mountain. Presently one of the merchants remarked that they were ruined.

'No use going home,' said the other.

Silence for a while and then:

'There is nothing to do, I suppose, but to turn robbers ourselves.'

'I wouldn't know how to begin.'

More silence.

'Why not begin on those fellows who got our pony. They weren't armed.'

So they ran up the hill by a short cut, and jumped out shouting they were robbers as the horse came panting through the pass. The others ran, and the merchants drove the pony up the mountain and home.

That is the way they are, but under provocation they can become formidable.

We had disorders in the country and disorders in town. One man was not enough to attend to them all. There was a seething under it all of the same discontent in various forms. Some of it had found expression in the Independents' movement in Seoul while I was still in the legation.

Led by former students of the American mission schools, a large number of patriots drew up a petition to the emperor asking for reforms and sat for days before the great gate of the palace. Some misguided person in the palace urged the emperor to use troops to disperse them and that opinion was supported by many. It was also suggested that it would be even better if the emperor did not take the appearance of suppressing reformers, and particularly since these people had the sympathy of the missionaries. So the pedlars' guild was called in. These people were really pedlars carrying small goods the whole length and breadth of the land. Some astute politician ages before had seen possibilities in them and organized them with their own laws and exemptions. They even imposed and executed the death penalty within their guild. The condemned man was placed in the middle of a circle of members and at a signal all would strike him on the head with the long cudgel every pedlar carried, all at the same time, so that no one of them would have his death on his conscience. They had become so useful as news gatherers and so powerful as messengers for conspirators that even royal princes sought to head the pedlars' guild, and finally it was abolished officially as dangerous, though it still lived. Word was sent to them that they would be reinstated in favour if they would drive the Independents out of town. That was hailed with enthusiasm, and groups of sturdy and resolute-looking cudgel bearers began to herd the groups of Independents to the river gate. Taken by surprise the latter ran out into the villages beyond to enlist slingers on their side, hotly followed by the pedlars. As the last of the pursuers passed through, heavy guards of soldiery were placed at every gate so that neither party could come back. In the meantime a beautiful battle had developed along the low line of hills toward the river. Korean villagers are expert stone throwers and still use the sling with great accuracy at long distances. Stone fights are a common sport between villages till the first death or serious casualty on either side. A heavy body of throwers and slingers advances, and behind them another group of cudgel men with helmets, shields, and body armour of twisted straw rope. The throwers rush the opposite party, and if the enemy weakens, the throwers spread out and the cudgel men charge in. The river villagers had come to the rescue of the Independents, and the pedlars were caught between thousands of stone throwers moving up from the river, and the bayonets of the troops behind them. There was nothing for them to do but fight it out. Every leader on both sides knew me, so there was no danger of an intentional accident. Both sides urged me, however, to keep out of reach of stones for it had to be fought out, and they placed me on a small hill with a group of men to guard me. Suddenly down in the thickest of the mob I heard a shot and a shout in English for help, with wild yells for vengeance rising above the general roar. I managed to get in and haul out a strange American who had been caught in the mess, had no idea what it was all about, and had shot a Korean, fortunately only through the fleshy upper part of the leg, so I was able to save both men. Then the battle joined in earnest. A leader went down under the cudgels, and a hundred men stamped furiously on him till he was unrecognizable. A small side mob dragged out what was left of him, wrapped it in straw mats, soaked the bundle in kerosene and burned it. It was the wrong way to handle a petition for reforms which everybody knew were needed, but it was typical of palace politics.

The dispersed and outlawed Independents' party was angered, where it might have been a valuable instrument of administration. If it had not been for the Russo-Japanese war a revolution might easily have come from them, just as it threatened from them for a while after the

Japanese occupation, when anti-Japanese activity was suspected among American missionaries, from whom the Independent leaders drew their political ideas and their ideas of reform. They were patriots and some of them excellent men, but when later I came into the Korean court it was quite impossible to use them in any way; the emperor's mind had been completely poisoned against them.

There were echoes of this trouble throughout the provinces to the remote back country where there were still rumblings of the Tong Hak rebellion which had been supressed so few years before that soldiers were still bringing in Tong Haks for execution when I first came to Seoul, and Tong Hak heads were hung by their long hair to the centre of three poles leaned together like a tepee, at the principal city gates where all could see them. It became difficult to tell political rebels from common bandits. Most of the single highwaymen who terrorized some districts were simply people who were hungry or had been driven into the hills by administrative abuses. There was nothing in Korea of the gang hooliganism we have in the United States. There were always reasons for disorder. With very little help the reasons could have been eliminated.

A dangerous feature of the situation was eternal interference by foreigners every time these troubles began to die down. One was fairly sure of catching a Japanese or two disguised in Korean dress, in any drive that captured these insurgents. As surely as one caught a Japanese some official from the nearest consulate would turn up to demand his extradition. It was never of the slightest use to attempt to take it up officially, for the Koreans could not raise their courage to make a protest. It was simpler to release the trouble-makers. In that regard the Japanese were every bit as troublesome as Americans have been in Nicaragua and other places in Central America where they have joined in or started revolutions, and I thought harshly of Japanese trouble-makers till I lived in Central America. What I feared greatly was the growth in Korea of some consolidation of these various discontented elements into a general movement like that of the Boxers which was growing to a head in China. That is why I wanted to be known to the people personally as widely as possible as being sympathetic with their troubles and at the same time determined that there should be no more violence, and went to the country on some pretext whenever I was free from palace duty.

In the northern provinces there was still another danger. Manchuria was really bandit-ridden. The Hung-Hutzes ('Red-beards' or riding robber bands) were evidently finding hard going at home under Russian pressure, for they were raiding across our border, plundering villages, driving off cattle, and looting crops. All the forest region of the Yalu and Tumen Rivers which form the northern frontier was uneasy and excited, and the raids were pushing in more boldly all the time. It was an unexplored region of high mountains and real forest, sparsely inhabited and totally unpoliced. It began to be necessary to do something about it, for if the Russians undertook to defend the border that would set the Japanese on fire.

I began to be aware also that there was an organization in that quarter that was lacking everywhere else. There was a head somewhere, and gradually I began to suspect that there were subheads, some of them this side of the border. It would do no good to ask for authority from the palace or to disclose my plans. There were too many mysterious channels of communication to the north and south, and our general staff, a useless group of stoutish elderly civilians in ill-fitting uniforms, would not know what to do. If I said anything in Seoul I would be stopped at once. We had some scattered army posts along the border line, in fearfully isolated spots. They were probably unofficered, for it was nobody's business to inspect them, and officers if assigned to duty there could not be expected to remain nearer to their garrison than the nearest town. I wanted some reasonably competent youngsters who would not be afraid of a winter in complete loneliness, to whom I could not even promise a reward if they did well. In what I proposed to do we might all get into trouble.

I confided in Gen. Ye Hak Kiun. The little general, who was not robust and was not supposed by his friends to be over-courageous, delighted me by joining up completely and enthusiastically with half a dozen of his best young officers. He was so keen that he started on ahead for Euiju, a border town on the lower Yalu, to wait for me there.

From what I could piece together out of scraps of gossip and misinformation the brains behind the raiding parties over the Manchurian border were those of that same young man who afterward became famous not only in Manchuria but beyond the boundaries of China, the great war lord, Chang Tso Lin. From an astute manipulator of robber bands he became a guerilla partisan leader and a person to be considered during the Russo-Japanese war; a person who could do things and hide his tracks, and he was courted by both the Russians and the Japanese. In China's civil war he became one of the most important of the great war dukes. He was credited with imperial ambition, and was assassinated as he withdrew his army from Peking to Mukden.

In my time he was not known and only beginning to be suspected. Gossip had it that he had Korean lieutenants on our side of the border, one of whom was identified to me as a man who had displayed considerable intelligence and strategic ability. His name had been connected with banditry and even with rebellion, but aside from these food raids of the Manchus, nobody knew just what he was trying to do. It might be just cattle rustling, it might be more serious, for he had been a leader among the Tong Hak rebels. It might be a general conspiracy.

It was believed that the mysterious Manchu chieftain himself had crossed over into Korea several times to meet this Korean and might again, and I proposed quite simply to catch him on our side and hang him, once and for all, and completely. I did not approve of hanging Koreans and never had part in condemning any, but a Manchu chief of the riding robbers was quite different, if I could catch him. If I could not, I meant to show him at least that we had teeth, and to leave my name and address where he could find them.

I had been able to arrange my absence from the city without attracting attention. It was custom in Korea that no one who had seen death might enter the palace for one hundred days – he was unclean and I had seen death recently. I was barred from the palace, and a visit of inspection to the northern provinces was approved. It was approved, that is, by the emperor, but not at all by Pavlow, the Russian minister. Ordinarily he was pleasant, but became quite violent when I told him I was going. He had some pointed remarks to make about American adventurers intruding where they were not wanted, from which I deduced that there might be some truth in the rumour brought to me that he had recently proposed to the Japanese government to divide Korea between them; the Russians to take the north with Peng Yang city, and the Japanese the south with Seoul. It seemed all the more necessary to find out what was happening in the north and if the great forests sheltered Cossacks as well as robbers.

I made haste to join General Ye at Euiju, by coasting steamer to Chinnampo, thence by native pony, changing every thirty miles. For some reason I was feeling badly. I was perplexed by the whole situation, but also I was feverish and my head ached intolerably. I pushed on to

An-ju, the ruined capital of one of the ancient kingdoms out of which Korea grew, and beyond into the mountains. I was travelling light: my soldier servant, Chang Sik, a fine youngster who spoke English, and a ruffianly Chinese cook. The cook gave me a good illustration of those ways that are dark and tricks that are vain, for which the heathen 'Chinee' is peculiar. I had felt too badly to try to live on the native food and had sent out for a Chinese who could cook and ride. A man was brought to me who would not stir unless I paid him double wages, for he was leaving home to go with me, and wife and children who must be supported in his absence. I promised, and gave him half the agreed sum for his family before starting. When we reached Euiju, opposite a flourishing Chinese town on the other side of the Yalu, he came to me to know if I wanted my linen properly washed and ironed, as he lived in that Chinese town, and his wife knew how to do foreign clothes. I had paid the rascal double wages for going home, not for leaving home.

From An-ju on I pressed forward as fast as the little post horses could carry my weight and soon left my men far behind. At the last village before a long stretch of wild road, there were no fresh horses to be had, but, though it was late, I was too ill to sleep then and decided to try to get through and strike the next village early in the morning.

Along toward midnight my plucky little horse gave out and fell. It was bitter cold, and clear moonlight, and looked a most favourable place for wolves. I looked about for some sign of human life, thought I could make out a miner's hut far up the mountain side and hailed it. Presently a light appeared and a miner came down toward me, with a little paper lantern. He studied me all over without a word, examined the horse, made me a sign to wait and presently returned with a load of heavy floor mats which he put under the horse and over him, finally covering him with bundles of straw.

'Wolves?' I asked.

'*Ahni!* (no) Not yet; snow come, wolves. No wolves, no *horangi* (tiger) yet.'

Then he signed to me to follow and we went up to his tiny one-room hovel. He seated me on the warmest part of the heated floor and offered me rice in a grimy brass bowl, evidently the unfinished half of his meal. I ate, for many of the country people had the same rule as desert Arabs about the temporary protection of a person who eats with them. Then he wiped the brass mouthpiece of his pipe and gave it to me, relighting the cold dottel.

'You are from the city?' he queried.

'Yes.'

'You are the adviser?'

'Yes.'

A very long pause, in which he studied me completely while I puffed at his very bitter pipe.

'You are a long way from the capital. It must be nation's business.'

I decided to try something on him.

'It is a nation's business. I am looking for . . .' (giving the name my scout had told me as the principal Korean lieutenant of the Manchurian marauders). I could see by his expression that he knew the name.

'Is he a great man?' he asked again.

'He is a strong man and, I think, a good man. I want to talk to him about Korea. I cannot say what I wish. I will tell you when the *chusa* comes.'

We sat for hours till all at once we heard voices in the distance and the hoof beats of horses on the frozen ground down in the pass, and exclamations as my men found my horse and loud calls for me.

'Your people?' said my host. I nodded.

'Soldiers?'

I shook my head and held up one finger. He opened the tiny window and set the lighted paper lantern in it. I had begun to suspect who he might be, but presently I knew it. My soldier stormed into the hut and threw up his rifle at my host. I knocked it aside.

'But master! he is the man!'

Turning to my young interpreter I told him:

'Say that I was looking for help and found it; that I found food and shelter, safety and courtesy. Say that I need help in Korea's needs. I cannot save Korea when Koreans help foreigners from across the border to make disorder. If it goes on I shall have to bring troops, and I do not want Koreans to kill Koreans. I want peace and that is the message I came to give the man we were talking about before you came. Let him go to him and tell him that. I want peace, but I can fight.' I was not trying to destroy any intelligence I might find; I wanted to tame it and use it.

We reached Euiju where the railway now crosses the Yalu, and I was lifted off my horse with a raging fever, and taken to General Ye's quarters in the local barracks. He had prepared a hut for me. My people spread out a straw mat on the hard mud floor, put a wooden block under my head for a pillow, spread a blanket over me, and waited for me to die. Some young officers came in occasionally with singing girls and public dancers to cheer me with music. General Ye, in one of my lucid moments, took down my address at home, to notify them of my death. A remote garrison up the river sent down a case of Cyrus Noble whisky they had ordered for a New Year's celebration. Harry Fessenden Meserve, the manager of Leigh Hunt's gold mines down country, sent some more and some tentative medical supplies, and I lived on whisky and raw eggs. I could not eat the native food even to live. It was cooked in castor oil and was served by the owner of the hut, a woman with some horrible disease that had eaten off her nose and lips and around her eyes till she looked like a living death's head. She was quite cheerful about it, and told me that her husband and children were all that way too. It was hard to separate her and the dancing girls from all the other bad dreams that went crowding through my aching head. During waking moments, for which General Ye watched patiently, we distributed our officers along the border posts and got the garrisons to show their teeth to the Manchu raiders. There was no sign of Russians, but there were Japanese who from their description were not coolies or pedlars. I was only active in spots. Ye did the work, consulting me when I looked sane, for most of the time I could not move and was not conscious of anything but pain.

It was a great relief when my soldier-servant foundered a good horse to reach an American passing some sixty miles away, who turned out to be a doctor. It was he who told me I had typhoid and might live since I had survived so long without him, if I would consent to be carried down country to his home and be nursed by him and his wife; bless all missionaries and their wives! I mended rapidly under their care, but most ungratefully broke his strict orders and ran away one night to try to get back to Euiju. It was no use. I fell off my horse and lay in the ditch until some miners carried me to their hut and notified the garrison that I was dead. I was awakened by the little general with a funeral procession come to bury me, and he put me in a carrying chair and sent me back to Seoul— so I never hanged Chang Tso Lin.

CHAPTER XI

THE AMAZONS

THE Boxer outbreak was in full blast. The Allies were slowly fighting their way up from Tientsin and no one knew if the beleaguered legations and missionaries in Peking were alive or dead. As a gesture, to impress the Koreans as well as Europe with the friendly attitude of the emperor toward the Western nations, I had chartered a steamer, loaded it with the only things we had to offer, rice and cigarettes, and sent it to the allied troops. I was not in the least sure, however, that some anti-foreign spark might not be fanned to a blaze on our side and watched everything that happened. Returning from one of my expeditions into the country I learned that word had come up from the island of Quelpaert of what seemed a formidable rebellion. A Catholic mission had been caught by it. Many people had been killed and there was a rumour of a massacre of Christians. Two small French gunboats, *l'Alouette* and *la Surprise*, had happened into Chemulpo harbour too late to take part in the China operations and had set off at once to the island. I had a sinking feeling that they might want to make up on our people for lost opportunity to bombard the Chinese Boxers, if French missionaries had been hurt.

There was a small Korean coasting steamer in Chemulpo; the nearest troops I could find who were not quite useless were one hundred Kang Wha men. I had to take their captain (a Seoul politician), but added several of the young Japanese trained officers from the military academy; got my interpreter Ko Hei Kiung to come along and raced the French gunboats. I knew they had not docked for a long time and hoped for even fouler bottoms than my own disreputable little tramp.

Coming from Japan to China by way of Fusan, the southernmost Korean port, Quelpaert looms up as a great blue volcanic cone, lying to the southwest of the steamer's course. It is well out of the way of all liners. It only serves to whet the curiosity of the traveller by its mystery before it fades out gradually as the liner rounds the lower end of the Korean peninsula and pokes into the tangle of currents and rocks and sea-washed mountains, which gave the emperor of Korea the title of lord of ten thousand isles and, less romantically, constitute a menace to navigation. I was glad of the chance to see and explore this island, in spite of my anxiety. It is not known even how the name of Quelpaert originated since the native name is Ché-ju. On old Chinese or Japanese maps it is indicated as the island of women. In recent years its only European visitors had been some rare missionary who had wandered over from the mainland only to be promptly expelled, or some surveying party landed from a passing man-of-war, which did its work as quickly as possible in the face of plain hostility and got aboard again. It was known only that the coast was so difficult and the inhabitants so unfriendly that even the Korean steamship company never landed there, but ran in a boat as near as they dared at long intervals, to take on from local junks whatever cargo the weather permitted, of dried fish, mother-of-pearl shell and thick-skinned bitter shattuck fruit. What trade there was in these things, and in potash got from seaweed, was carried to market mainly by the stout little craft of Japanese smugglers, half junk, half schooner, or in the frail native fishing boats, fastened together with wooden bolts and carrying sails of straw matting, which are drawn up on the shore well out of reach of the sea when the weather threatens. The Japanese smugglers had buttressed their own trade by fostering anti-European feeling on the one hand, and the old local feeling of independence from Korea on the other. Because of its isolation, the island was used by Seoul as a penal colony for political prisoners. It was nominally administered from Seoul but only nominally, for not only this tradition of independence but another curious custom made it a difficult place to govern. Man, in this lost corner of the world, was the inferior being; the woman was everything. She was the real house-bond. She owned all the property; her children bore her family name, and she never took a permanent husband. Men were allowed to come over from the mainland once a year, but were not encouraged to stay long, and when they returned, took with them all boys who had reached thirteen years. A few men lived in the three cities, almost as foreigners lived in the open ports of China, on sufferance. These and the political priosners made up the whole male population, and the women dominated the life of the island even in public matters. It was more than a matriarchy; it was a real Amazon community, for the women were always ready to assert their power and uphold it by force. These two traditions were so strong that the governor sent down from Seoul was never permitted to bring his wife with him, lest a son born in the palace of the native kings, which was his official residence, should lay claim to the throne of the island kingdom, which he would have the right to do. The natives did not want a Korean king, nor the Koreans a king of Quelpaert, so the custom suited both.

The political exiles could not leave the island, but were otherwise free and unsupervised. They could live where they liked and make their living as they pleased.

The native men were hunters, fishers, coast traders and smugglers. They stayed away from the women as much as possible, either at sea or in the mountain forest, and left all land work to them.

The rocky volcanic soil gave scanty crops of millet, and that only in fields built up of boulder walls filled with earth carried in baskets. Nearly all cereal food was brought sixty miles from the nearest point on the mainland, often a week's journey through the twisting currents and the rough sea which prevailed along that part of the coast.

The women were fine swimmers and divers. Young and old would swim out through the breakers, leave a basket buoyed by gourds floating on the surface and dive fathoms down for abalone shell or a bunch of edible seaweed. They would cut it out with a short sickle (the same weapon they used on the men when annoyed), attach an empty gourd to it, drop the stone with which they had weighted the gourd and let it float to the surface to be picked up when they were ready to come up themselves. They could swim and float about for hours, dive as simply as a duck, and work or move about from place to place under the water as easily and as long as so many sea fowl. While resting on the surface they would keep up a monotonous whistling in different keys to warn chance men in the fishing boats to keep their distance.

The island is obviously a volcano. All around the coast are sunken, needle-pointed reefs. The foreshore is the same formation and almost impossible to walk on except by the worn trails. The whole island rises abruptly through chains of foothills to the crater of Hanra-San (pronounced Halla-San), the Mt. Auckland of our maps, 6,558 feet high.

The 'dragon's gates,' two great rifts, fall from the top of the mountain to the northern and southern coasts. Over their beds of lava, small streams flow which were said to come from a lake in the crater. There were hunters who claimed to have seen the lake, but it was a sacred and dangerous spot that most people avoided.

According to Korean history, which is so full of myths that it is difficult to judge the historic value of anything, in a vague year of an equally vague reign, a huge commotion took place in the sea off the southern coast, and a great mountain arose, spouting fire. When the flames had cooled, the three families of Ko, Pu and Yang came up from three caves and peopled the island as rulers, nobles and peasants, respectively. These first men, become demigods, still lived on the shores of the crater lake. Sometimes they allowed themselves to be seen, sometimes they punished the intruder.

The Ko family were the ancient kings of Quelpaert, which is exactly why I asked Ko Hei Kiung to go along, hoping that his name would weigh more heavily than a hundred ragamuffin soldiers with single-shot rifles salvaged from the Franco-Prussian war. His family, one of the most noble in Korea, still worshipped theoretically at the temple built over the entrance to the cave from which their founder came out to be king.

There are three cities on the island. The capital, Ché-ju, on the northern shore, raises its walls and towers almost from the water, all overgrown with ivy, centuries old, and its roofs nearly hidden by huge salisburia trees, pomegranates of extraordinary size, with groves of pummelo or shattuck, and bitter oranges.

Higher up on the slopes of the lava hills, groups of low houses appear, built of cobblestones and bits of lava, with heavy rocks and rope nets protecting the thatched roofs from the sea winds, like the cables stretched across Porto Rican roofs to hold them against hurricanes. Beyond are grassy slopes and higher still a thick tangle of bamboo and brier, a real jungle covering the higher peaks from Mt. Sarabon to Halla-San. There is plenty of game above, wild cattle, boar and deer, and wild ponies slender as deer, and with hoofs of iron from the jagged lava rocks. The islanders lasso them as needed and break them with a stout club, before shipping them to the mainland as tame.

Of the other two walled towns the important one was Tai-jung, as the seat of a sort of rival government. Tai-jung is evidently the 'Tadiane' of Hendrick Hamel, a Dutch trader who was wrecked not far from the town in the *Sparrow Hawk* in 1653. His description, under the title of 'Narrative of an Unlucky Voyage' is the only description that existed thirty years ago, and is accurate, for his errors can be identified as only misunderstanding. For example, he calls Ché-ju 'the town of Moggan or Moksa.' Evidently his captors told him they were taking him to the Mo-gwan or Moksa, that is, the governor, who has always had his residence in the old capital. Nothing had ever been published about this island except this Hamel narrative, and references to it in ships' logs, or a brief account of the adventures of two American missionaries who were landed and promptly expelled.

The 'Sailing Directions' for 1904, quoting from the survey of Capt. Sir E. Belcher, H.M.S. *Samarang*, state that 'the island is about forty miles long, seventeen in breadth, oval in shape and of great height, with only one anchorage for sailing vessels, at the east end between Quelpaert and Beaufort Island.'

In and around the three towns and in the narrow strip between sea and mountain lived a population computed by the Korean government at a hundred thousand. The Koreans had no basis at all for their calculation, mine was of the crudest, and as the British survey is undoubtedly correct the population was probably much lower than that, but with the whole island in unanimous rebellion, and one hundred unreliable men to restore peace and keep order, they certainly looked numerous.

No news of the uprising had leaked out through the Japanese in our direction, for those who frequented the island were of a type that is not in communication with its officials. These two priests apparently had met with great success in their mission, for there were still Christians on the island exiled during the great persecution and they had made many new converts. For some reason that was not yet clear, the insurgent movement had taken the form of a drive against the Christians, who had withdrawn to Ché-ju, and were defending the town under the leadership of the two priests. They had armed themselves, some of the townspeople and a handful of the governor's police, with antiquated weapons from the government arsenal, and were besieged by a wild mob estimated at ten thousand islanders, malcontents and brigands from the mainland.

That is what started the two French gunboats to the rescue. They beat my old tramp steamer in the race but by a margin too narrow to take control or do anything more than open communication with the missionaries and take aboard some Christians. I informed the French senior officer of my authority, and proceeded to land my men on the narrow water front, under the walls of a dead city. Hardly had the priests' messenger got through the blockade to the nearest telegraph office on the mainland, when the women of the town, fearing starvation, opened the city gates at night to the rebels and led a complete massacre of the defenders. Not a shot nor a sign of life came from the walls. The city gates hung wide open and the narrow streets were cumbered with dead bodies. I counted a group of ninety, young and old of both sexes, all horribly mutilated, before the governor's gate on the market place, where they had been lying for ten days in rain and sun. Not a living soul showed in the town till after we had entered, stored our provisions and ammunition, closed the gates and placed sentries on the walls. The two priests had survived. From one and a few eye-witnesses of the massacre I got the story of that night, ten days before. Everyone who had a grievance, public or private, or a debt, seized his opportunity and killed and looted, ally or enemy alike. When the destruction was complete, the victors withdrew from the town to the foothills to see what would happen next. Except the few

Christians who had escaped there was not a man in town. There was no one to bury the dead, and my soldiers would refuse to do it. I knew that and did not want to risk a mutiny right at the start. It was another week before I could capture and pay enough coolies to give the bodies decent burial, and I had to live just where they were thickest, in the governor's palace. I found a room opening on the garden as far away from them as I could, but even there a wretched bird flew over my table and dropped a long mesh of hair in my food with a bit of skull attached. Outside the town masses of men showed up on all the hills to landward; all day long, after the first day and night, they kept a dropping fire of jingals and mediaeval bronze cannon, which generally fell short of the walls; every time I showed myself a quite recognizable rifle shot, a little more accurate, warned me not to stand too long in one place. Fortunately the average Japanese boatman is no better with foreign shooting weapons than the Koreans. All night, flames from some burning house or village the campfires all over the hills warned us that the seige might begin again if the rebel leaders found out how few we were. The presence of the *Surprise* and *Alouette* kept them in doubt until it was too late for them to act. Captain de Mornay was a thorough sportsman. As soon as I had got into the town he sent an officer to say that he yielded 'to Korean government authority' and left the situation in my hands. Having given his official message, the young officer asked if he might give a private one as man to man, and told me that the French officers were much concerned by the appearance and lack of discipline of my soldiers. They would withdraw the two gunboats if I required it, but would prefer to stand by in case of need. They did not quite like 'to leave a white man in such a mess.' He then brought out a bundle containing rockets and flares for use in an emergency at night and signal pennants for day use. They would either send in boats to

bring us off, give us a landing party to assist or throw a few
shells over toward the dense crowds on the hills, which
were quite visible to them with a telescope. They also
wanted to know if I were adequately armed 'even against
my own men' and well supplied with decent food. I did
not have to use their offer, but I was grateful for it and
much more comfortable about the result of my campaign. The first thing to do was to impress the watchers
outside that we had a military force and that it was alert,
so I had the whole hundred move about singly, as sentries
on the walls. Next, one of my young officers came and
told me that the commanding officer claimed to have
secret instructions not to fight. He was to withdraw if
there was any danger. He also reported that the soldiers
were discussing going off to the steamer and returning to
the mainland without their officers and leaving me there.
It began to seem that we must meet these simple souls
with guile. I sent our only vessel away and let them know
it had gone to bring more troops. The two French priests
and the acting governor had been saved as prisoners by
the influence of one of the political exiles, a Seoul man, a
leader in the local revolution, who had been implicated in
the murder of the queen in 1894. His wider experience
showed him that the killing of foreigners was a much
more serious matter than a simple revolt against unjust
taxation. It had also come out that the Christian massacre
was accidental to the real revolt, and not a primary factor.
Taxes in Quelpaert were sporadic. They were always
unpopular and rarely collected. Some years before my
time there had been a tax revolt and the collectors had
been driven off the island. An imperial proclamation then
had relieved the 'loyal islanders' of all back taxation, and
none had been collected since. Early in this year one of
that infernal tribe of go-getters, which is not confined to
the United States, had offered to the emperor to produce
a much-needed sum for the privy purse by collecting all

back taxes in Quelpaert, including those remitted years before. On arrival he had invented some new ones in addition. When the islanders objected he discovered that in former times he had been a follower of a French missionary and joined up again with the Christians; it was even alleged that, unknown to the priests, he had promised exemption from taxes for native Christians. When the revolt came he had a place of refuge and Christianity became an issue in the fighting. We promptly suppressed the tax collector who was only too glad to get away, and I got a message to the Seoul exile, through one of my faithful servants, that I was grateful to him for his intervention on behalf of the missionaries, and could say the same on behalf of the French legation, and that I would remember it when I began to wipe out the insurgents. I also let him know that heavy reinforcements were on the way, but that I did not propose to wait for them. My man was instructed to let it drop that I was an ambitious young person who did not want the general arriving with the new troops to take credit for suppressing the revolt, so I might be expected to attack at any moment with what men I had, who were plenty to handle undisciplined mobs. My man was also to say in the course of his gossip that I was asking the Japanese government to send over and arrest any Japanese who might be on the island, suspecting that anyone there would not face the risk. I further let it be known that before starting a general slaughter I wanted assurance that Mr Ko would be unmolested if he went out to worship at the shrine of his ancestors, as everybody realized was his duty, and which it would be sacrilege to prevent.

Through the same young officer-conspirator who arranged the messages, I organized drills outside the walls, for the besiegers were getting courage and coming down too close. The commanding officer was not at all inclined to show his ignorance by drilling the men; I had it pointed out to him that it was very dangerous not to drill them, for if they remained idle they might quite easily mutiny and kill us all. In his innocence he turned the drill over to the lieutenant. My lieutenant opined that if anybody hurt our ruffians they would fight. So we took them for a walk outside the walls hoping for the worst. We drilled up and down the countryside with fixed bayonets at the double, none of the hostile groups waited for us to come up, and none of the Japanese snipers hit me. It was comic opera, perhaps, but when I thought of that I also thought of the look of the shambles through which we had passed the day we landed. Presently the poison I had sent out in my messages began the work. The exiled leader saw visions of amnesty because of his intervention on behalf of the priests and the governor. Then more messages went out, addressed to no one in particular, just memoranda in which I discussed with myself the utility of executing certain leaders named in the paper as against the guarantee of trial if they surrendered, with consideration of any extenuating circumstances, which I allowed to be lost and found by the rebels. That also had its effect and presently requests for private interviews began to come in. Once negotiations had started, I felt they could be kept alive till the arrival of the two hundred and fifty trained troops I had sent for.

As soon as I believed that these could not be very far off I got out a proclamation, warning the people of the island that I was about to begin a drive with my soldiers, so that all honest men might remain indoors. In it I said that the emperor would listen to grievances, and a committee might come in to present them, but that my special object was to catch the leaders of the revolt, whose names were all in my possession, though even to these I would guarantee a fair trial by the supreme court at Seoul.

I announced that if these chiefs surrendered voluntarily it would be in their favour. If they were brought in prisoners by loyal subjects, the latter would be remembered; but I added that in any case the revolt was now over and I intended to clean up the guilty immediately, before the new troops arrived, in order to avoid unnecessary bloodshed. It was not such a long chance, for the two gunboats still hovered off the coast, as near as weather permitted, and the islanders all knew what they were, even if they did not know that they were not Korean and part of my force. Negotiations were well on, when a pompous and much uniformed colonel turned up with the regiment I had asked for. A number of leaders gave themselves up: some were arrested, and the rest fled in Japanese fishing boats.

We arranged then for a surrender of the whole rebel army. They were to come in and deliver their weapons, listen to an address from our gallant and imposing colonel, and go home. The two gunboats left; the priests settled down and reopened their mission, and I put thirteen principal captives on board my steamer, perfectly free of the ship and only under guard on the way up to Seoul, when we reached port.

The final grand tableau of my little comic-opera war was really impressive. Thousands of rebels came in; I could only estimate them in their huddled masses. They were armed with prehistoric weapons. Some wore armour made of iron plates fastened to a cumbersome leather tunic or to a quilted and wadded cotton cloak. Some were dressed in leather cloaks with hairy dog-skin hats, like the coon-skin caps of American pioneer riflemen, the tail of the dog dangling over the shoulders. Some had bows and iron-tipped arrows; others had the usual Korean matchlock guns. Many had spears and flails, made of a short cudgel studded with iron points fastened by two interlocking rings to a long staff. There were many jingals, those long-barrelled Malay and Chinese fortress guns, which have to be laid on a wall or a heap of rocks to fire them, and are loaded with a handful of slugs, scrap iron or stones. There was a museum collection of small bronze hand cannon, of great age. They were real cannon, of Chinese origin, big enough to carry an impressive load, and small enough to be taken from place to place on the back of one man or even one small one in each hand. Also, there were some shotguns of Japanese make and a Murata army rifle, of the latest model. A hundred well-disciplined native soldiers under trustworthy officers would have had no trouble with them, even with thousands of them, for they had nothing that could come within range even of the wretched Berdan and Gras survivals of 1870 that a French government had permitted to be sold for the equipment of the Korean army. My hundred tatterdemalions with their smarter city reinforcements looked like an army and like real soldiers beside these island scarecrows. My weakness was treachery within, rather than rebel numbers. An added weakness always was my unwillingness to use force with the Koreans. I was trying to save and rebuild.

After the surrender, I left them in the hands of the colonel and the new governor who had come down with him, after a full understanding with them that there were to be no reprisals and no taxes levied until a new tax law had been worked out and a commission sent down from Seoul to explain it.

I have always been sorry that the weeks I spent in Quelpaert were so full of other things that I had no chance to explore it. My visit there was probably the last of the Amazon tradition. A garrison remained until the Japanese occupation of Korea. After that, it is said, the island was fortified by the Japanese government, and where their fortresses exist there is no exploring. Unless the missionaries gather something of its history, Quelpaert will remain a mystery as it was before.

The sequel to the war was the trial of the rebel leaders

at Seoul. I wished it to be an exemplary trial. It should be the first illustration of the new order of justice in Korea. Beyond presenting a report to the emperor of the reasons of the revolt, what had happened and the circumstances under which the accused were presented for trial, I intended to have no part in it except to sit as an observer with the Korean judges and to see to it that the men had a proper defence and that witnesses were admitted in their favour as well as against them. The French legation asked for and obtained the privilege of having a representative present, because of the attack on the French missionaries. I did not like that. I wanted a Korean trial, without any feature that could be construed as foreign pressure. Next, the local Japanese reporters asserted a right to be present. They had no such right, of course, but I would have permitted it, for I wanted them to hear whatever evidence might be produced as to the presence of Japanese among the rebels or at the massacre of Christians. I suspected strongly that their wish to hear what was going on came from the same reason and might be connected with those Murata rifle bullets which were noticeable whenever I appeared on the walls and were never wasted on Korean soldiers.

I wanted their legation to ask as the French had done through the proper channels that they might be present, but they would not do that and the reporters and some soshi forced the door of the judges' room where we were in private session, terrifying the native policemen on duty and throwing the judges into panic, for they were armed with sword canes, the usual Japanese civilian weapon. I explained once more that there were ordinary decencies to be observed, and when they still insisted on breaking up the court I threw them out personally and vigorously, which was the beginning of a new rabid newspaper campaign against me extending to the Tokyo press.

I was disappointed in the efficiency of our new model of justice. Seeing that I did not intend to try them myself, and would not testify though I knew their cases, so as to give them every possible chance, accused and witnesses looked me blandly in the eye and lied brazenly. Finally the chief justice turned to me and said that though he hated to disrupt the course of Western justice, he felt that an ever so slight return to primitive methods might give better results, and asked if he might threaten to use the paddle. It seemed to me that if he threatened it might show the prisoners that they had better not force the issue, and I consented to his ordering the paddles brought out, if he promised to accept defeat if they called his bluff, in which case I would agree to testify. The court servants brought out a kind of saw-buck over which the victim was to be held while being spanked, and the paddles. The effect was instantaneous. They all clamoured to be readmitted to examination as they had remembered something. The instruments were removed and the trial finished in an orderly manner, but it was the last trial on the Western model as well as the first.

Quelpaert brought two interesting new acquaintances. Admiral Pottier with his flagship *Redoutable* was a figure of the eighteenth-century sea fighters. Under his sea-wolf bluster he was a shrewd diplomat, and under his weather-beaten skin he was a man of peace. He got for me the Cross of the Legion of Honour for preventing the bombardment of the island by his own ships and for keeping Korea out of the Boxer movement. When detailed to the China station to close a long career of diplomacy and action in the Mediterranean, he had selected as his flagship the oldest of old French ironclads, for he detested the discomforts of the new mechanical fighting machines. His quarters were fitted like a Paris apartment, and across the stern he had run out nothing less than a glassed balcony where he raised flowers. Ladies, when lunching or dining with the admiral (and he entertained like an ambassador), were warned by his aides that they must under no circumstances understand half of what he said, for he had a queer trick of speech, filling his brilliant conversation not only with hair-raising oaths but with quite impossible barrack-room terms, at which, if a lady took offence, she proved herself no lady, for she had no business to understand them. He was served aboard by a civilian butler-valet who had sailed with him, according to the tale, for over forty years, and with whom he stood in relations only possible with an old French or Italian family servant. The old valet had been with the admiral through all his most intimate experiences, and kept a stern eye on the admiral's stories.

'Admiral, you exaggerate,' would come suddenly from the background, 'You know it happened *this* way—'

A spluttering of oaths from the admiral, and a fiery debate between the two old men was sure to follow, during which the service halted and the guests, if they knew the peculiarities of their host, rocked with delight. The old gentleman was a museum piece; he belonged at least a century back, for even his shrewd and kindly wisdom belonged to the great period of territorial rather than commercial empire building. He belonged with Clive.

On his staff was a Commander Vignaud, better known as Pierre Loti, a short little man, with high heels to give him stature, corsetted tightly as a belle of former days, cheeks and lips rouged like a modern flapper. It was incredible that any man could live under such studied rudeness and contempt as that of the sturdy Breton officers of the flagship. They disliked his effeminacy as only a blue-water sailor can detest such things; they studied the insults in which they expressed their feelings as only a French courtier could – to remain well within bounds of civilized intercourse while making life unbearable for one whom they quite plainly believed to be unfit for the company of men. Yet it surely cannot be said that Bretons have no appreciation of the soul of a poet. Perhaps they prefer him bearded and bardlike.

The admiral did not even trouble to be civil. His language about Pierre Loti and to him was unstudied and without reserve.

CHAPTER XII

NATIVE TRUST AND HOSPITALITY

THE traveller in Korea soon learned that medical missionaries set an embarrassing standard for all other Americans, for all came to be looked upon in the back country as powerful medicine men. When suffering people came for help, one simply had to do something about it. Koreans were considered shy and suspicious of foreigners; I always found them trusting, and hospitable as the Arab of fiction.

For all its healthy climate, Korea was full of disease. Typhoid and typhus were endemic. Smallpox was so common that we lost all fear of it. Contagious eye diseases gave the mission doctors more practice and skill than they could get in a lifetime at home, and once in a while cholera swept down on us from China like a hurricane. In those times of public need the Koreans turned to the Americans, and most of us turned to and lent a hand.

One summer I was riding up in the North, near the American gold-mining concession. It was hard going, for the rains were heavy and the rivers were out. One of my most valued men was drowned from a small boat below Peng Yang in a specially treacherous river. I called to him something from the river bank; in his rigid code of etiquette he stood up while I was speaking and lost his balance. We found him twenty miles down the river two weeks later. A young Korean who joined our party for safety stepped into the river at An-ju, was washed away and disappeared. We never found him, though we delayed our journey and searched. Crossing in small boats and swimming our horses on a leash, we landed on a broad expanse of sand in which footprints showed going toward the city water gate. Our men on foot got through to the higher ground. I rode in the centre on a heavy horse and behind came my companion and the pack caravan of light Korean ponies. Suddenly I felt myself standing on my feet, though still in the saddle and realized that we had at last got into the quicksands for which we watched at every river crossing. Men on foot who knew the place could pass quickly without breaking the crust, but a large party like mine had disturbed the surface and my big horse had gone through. I shouted to the caravan behind to scatter wide, climbed over the horse's head to an unbroken part, and eventually got out. The crust broke under the horse's weight exactly like the ice on a skating pond.

At our next river we were all so demoralized that we camped and waited for the water to go down. While we were sitting there, an old woman came through higher up and implored us to help her husband who had been terribly burned. I was ashamed not to try to pass a flood that had not stopped an old grandmother. I took all I had in the way of remedies: a sheet, a bottle of carbolic acid and a can of vaseline, and went with her wishing myself well out of it. The straw thatch of the old couple's hovel had caught fire and fallen in, burning the man's back to a crisp from neck to waist. The flies had got into it and hatched, and it looked gangrenous. I could not back out, so I sharpened my knife to a razor edge and shaved away everything down the clean flesh, while my patient lay and smoked his long pipe, without a whimper. I still am not sure whether there are any large veins in that part of a man's anatomy, but if there are I missed them. I soaked him in a strong solution of carbolic and covered him thick with vaseline, and ran back to camp as if I had been murdering. Several weeks later when I came again that way, old Philemon and Baucis came out bearing thank offerings of eggs and chickens; my patient had made a perfectly healthy cure. Not all countrymen were so guileless. Once, I was riding one of the Chasseurs d'Afrique Arabs given to the emperor by General Voyron, a horse built like a greyhound, all chest and no middle. When I tried to mount without stirrups, after crossing a river, the saddle turned and he bucked away to the next village leaving a trail of coffee, sugar and Winchester cartridges from the saddle bags. I asked at the village if anyone had seen a horse.

'A horse you call that?' chorused the village elders – 'a tiger, a flying dragon! He is not a horse!'

'Medius' has been going so fast that at the turn of the street he had gone straight on, through a window and into a tiny room where two oldest inhabitants were playing checkers. The horse was wedged in, the old men crouched in corners to get away from his heels and the tea cups were mostly in splinters in his hide. He had ruined my saddle, broken my rifle and cast all four shoes, so having started him back home on a halter, I called for an estimate of the damages. There was so much doubt about it that I told the village headman to let me know on my way home in two weeks' time. When I passed that way again, there was a heap of broken crockery in the street a yard high and a bill a yard long, in which everybody in the village was to share; but that village was nearer the capital and sophistication.

There was certainly more luck than good management in this amateur practice of medicine. One of the Americans who had just married and brought out a perfectly inexperienced wife had to go on duty to some place where he could not take her and asked me to look in once in a while and see that she was safe. One day I went to their house. Not a servant answered the gate and no one seemed to be in the house. I went through and found the poor girl in bed, deserted, only half conscious, and with a horrible case of confluent smallpox, black smallpox, we called it. Carbolic acid and vaseline were the only remedies I knew anything about, but they seemed to do until we found a doctor, and she got well. The worst part came when she wanted a looking glass to see what had happened to her and I was afraid to give it. I was wrong, for she took it like a hero. My native servants always surprised me in these cases. They never hesitated a second to go where I wanted to go, nor to stay alone if I asked it, even with contagious disease.

The great cholera epidemic which struck the Philippines and spread all up the China coast caught us without warning. One morning forty men were dead in a cell of the central prison. The cell was built for twelve, but forty-eight had been crowded in. The jail was built on the main sewer canal and drained into it. Women washed their food and washed their clothes in the canal and threw their refuse there. At night countrymen came in to carry off loads of the black muck to spread on the market gardens and raise the cucumbers and melons that everybody ate in the streets. There was no doubt that an epidemic must spread from the prison to the town. Dr Kitasato in Japan had just announced the discovery of a cholera serum. It had been entirely successful in the laboratory, but had never been tried generally. Through the Japanese legation we got several thousand doses, all that could be produced so hurriedly. It had to be administered in the small of the back in quantity that took an instrument as big as a garden syringe. Nobody would touch it unless I tried it first, so I submitted and it ruined me. I was feverish for weeks and so sore and lame that I could hardly mount or sit my horse. No one would go near the prison cell so I disinfected it myself with strong carbolic; I burned all clothes and blankets and scrubbed the eight survivors. Some one told me that sulphuric acid killed cholera and there was a good supply of that to be had, so I prepared a mild solution of it sweetened with sugar to make a sort of lemonade and made my prisoners drink it. No more died in that cell, even from my medicine. We cleaned up the entire prison in the same way and the epidemic died out there. I was certain it had gone through the sewer canal though, and sure enough it turned up all through the town first in isolated cases and then everywhere. Having been successful in my first cases I was put in charge of the epidemic by the emperor, though completely without knowledge of the disease, without drugs and with no funds to compensate the few doctors I could get to help. We organized the American missionaries in Peng Yang as an advisory board to the governor, for we had learned that one of the prisoners in the death cell had come straight over from China and through Peng Yang. It was more difficult in Seoul, for nobody, natives or foreigners, would pay the slightest attention to any rule. Only one of the foreign colony had ever seen a cholera epidemic, old Mr Stripling, formerly of Scotland Yard and for many years in the police service of India. He was supposed to be training the Seoul police force, but like most of these officers he was neither called on nor allowed to do anything real or practical. He told me of a pill used in India, made of opium and another ingredient which I have forgotten, to be administered on the first cholera symptoms, another in three hours, the third in two hours after that, when the patient would recover or die. An old French priest told me that no one who kept a nicotine solution in his mouth could possibly catch the cholera germ, for it enters only by the mouth and nicotine is as fatal to it as sulphuric acid. With this brilliant medical preparation, we fought the greatest epidemic in memory. Having cleaned the prison and dumped lime in the canal for good luck without knowing whether it would do any good or not, I used the rest of the Kitasato serum on the people most likely to be exposed, the letter carriers and police. The Japanese legation doctor, who ran an amateur medical school, turned himself and his students into a first-aid relief corps, using opium pills by the barrel. Wherever a case occurred we swabbed down the house as far as our disinfectants would go, and removed the inhabitants to one of our three concentration camps; that is, we did if they were poor people and helpless. The rich would not budge nor admit us. In the concentration camps I fed the poor victims on sulphuric acid lemonade, and in the course of time the epidemic slackened, flared up again and died as quickly as it came, after a good many thousands of deaths. Cholera is not a pleasant thing to watch. It is evidently more than ordinarily painful. I felt so badly about my patients and victims that I spent a good deal of my time with them, knowing that I was quite helpless but at least keeping up an appearance of helping them; for they were pathetically trustful, and in the guarded camps caused no trouble at all and always welcomed me, as they did the old French abbé who spent all his time going from camp to camp looking for his people. It was he who told me about the nicotine, which theory I later saw confirmed in some medical journal by the observation of a German physician during the cholera epidemic in Hamburg. The priest taught them to chew tobacco, although many of our missionaries were trying to abolish tobacco among their Christians. He had no cure to offer, but simply talked to them, sat with them, held dying men in his arms and soothed their relatives, but he had a wonderful influence. One evening, riding back from inspection, I heard a woman's wail of appeal from a hillside covered with graves and tombs. Under a rough shelter of straw matting lay her husband dead of cholera. She threw herself at our feet begging us to cure him.

'But he has been dead for days,' I said.

'Yes, lord, for more than a week, but there were no Americans, and now you have come and you will give him back to me!'

Those were really the hard spots, for she would not believe that her husband was far beyond cure, even though what was left of him was crying out for burial.

It was, as always, the foreigners who were hard to manage. Even the most sensible was jealous of any other nationality, and co-operation was hopeless. In Peng Yang we got action because the colony there was American and I was American. In Seoul the board of health I tried to set up to deal with the epidemic would do nothing suggested by anyone of another nationality and as a board was utterly useless. I notified the diplomats of the location of my concentration camps and of health conditions in a daily bulletin and asked their help in keeping the camps completely isolated. A word from them to the emperor supporting what I was trying to do for the general good would have been of the greatest moral value and might even have brought forth funds sufficient to do something. An immediate response to my appeal came from the Russian consul. At the bottom of my circular bulletin he noted that nobody had a right to exclude him from any place, and actually forced his way past my sentries at each camp in turn. If it had not been that in the growing struggle between Russia and Japan one had to weigh every act toward both in order not to appear to favour either at the expense of the other, I am sure that I would have had him arrested and tried the issue with the Russian minister. The Koreans were always afraid to raise any point about arbitrary acts of Japanese, so I swallowed a good deal from the Russians to keep the balance equal.

Another and a worse plague even than the cholera was what the Japanese called the pneumonic plague which decimated Manchuria frequently and once in a while struck across the border. Fortunately it never got as far south as Seoul. It seemed to be a swift disintegration of the lungs, and so catching that it was the only thing that really terrified us. All these other things were part of life. One got used to them. Even the cholera was not terrifying. One came home from sick rounds, stripped all clothes off and threw them in a strong disinfectant and took a complete disinfectant bath before going into the house, where food was kept carefully protected from flies. One took precautions, and that was all. No one knew what precautions to take against the Manchurian plague, and those who had to be in the north in winter were not happy.

The thing that held one up against the palace intrigues was the trust of the simple people, whether in help for their physical ills or any other trouble. Even though I never learned to talk to them fluently in their own language I had enough to make my own wants known and to understand theirs, and I am still sure that a strict supervision over their rulers and a lenient but consistent and honest rule for the mass of the people would have developed a fine race. There was no feeling of danger in travelling about the country such as there was in China or even in Japan. The Koreans could be vicious when driven too far, but I never experienced an unprovoked attack such as always lurked in the background in China and was a common thing even in Japan. I remember only one village where I ever met with actual hostility, and even then the villagers were only surly and refused to sell food either for me or for my horse. I got along for myself without it and fortunately had out one of my Arab horses, for they eat anything. I collected a lot of dried bean pods from the last harvest, boiled them till they were soft, and the horse ate the mess hot and went on quite fresh and happy.

At times I found village people suspicious when I had a following, for native officials took what they needed without paying. When I encountered that feeling, I paid in advance, and after a while I found often that they would not take pay, and I would have to send back a present from Seoul to make up for it. The great houses in the country were always hospitable. Travellers of noble rank were lodged in the house. Two buildings were set apart for others. In one, travellers of lower rank were housed, with food free. In the other, poor people were not only sheltered and fed but given food and rough shoes for the further journey and a small sum of money to carry them over the next stage. Food and lodging were always free in the monasteries, for as long as one wished to stay, though it was customary for people who could do it to leave a money gift.

The day's journey was one hundred li; ten li was an hour's walk at the gait that any old person or child could make it, about three and a third miles. Ponies went no faster, for one did not ride ponies; they were led by a groom on foot and one only sat perched on their high saddles to save one's steps.

Public inns were to be avoided. They were the sleeping places for beggars, lepers, and caravan drivers. All the men slept huddled on the warm floor in one room, while just outside, under an open shed, the ponies hung along a great trough squealing and fighting all night for remnants of food. They hung literally. A wide belt was passed under them and they were raised by it almost off their feet, to prevent injury by kicking. Gentling and training a horse seems never to have occurred to anybody. One had to be really tired to sleep in those places, for the stable shed was placed as near the men's quarters as possible because of tigers.

Travel was freer on foreign horses. One was not held to the sleeping places exactly a hundred li apart. In the hot season three in the morning was the time to break camp. With luck, by four, but usually by five, the day's journey was well begun, with a rest from eleven to two and a shorter march in the afternoon. By dark everyone was taking as much sleep as the cleanliness of his lodging allowed.

Those early-morning rides were delicious in spite of bad luck in the matter of vermin during the night. In the half darkness wild geese waddled about the field edges, almost under the horses' feet; pheasants sat like chickens where the first sun rays would strike the valley; deer would watch from the roadside quite unafraid. One morning, in a shallow valley, a thin mist over the fields and the sun just up above the hills, a flight of sacred ibis rose, all pink in the dawn. Dividing, one half rose in a circle high in the clear air, spread and then fell rapidly, while the others rose in a perfect ring through the wider circle of the first to the same height, to spread and drop in their turn, while the first rose through them again, all in a babble of calls and talking.

Along the side of the trail ran a little stream reddening everything it touched, pebbles and rocks and roots; bubbling with some natural gas. Two great slabs of granite stood out of the mist, a third laid across the top like some ancient place of sacrifice, and far off on a hillside ran a great wall with gate towers in which my people said there was nothing but a poor village and a few fields where once a royal town had been. Above the wall showed great chestnut trees, widespread like those that shade the Tartar villages in the Krimea. That night we lodged in a village off the main road, in the house of a young friend of the officer who rode with me, who was marrying that day. The bridegroom, hearing that we were coming, gave us the first use of his new dwelling, fresh and spotless, while he remained in his father's house for as long as we should stay. We had hardly entered before the courtyard and outer rooms were filled with the usual crowd of village gossips. Some wanted remedies for their troubles, some wanted to see a foreigner, feel his clothes, examine the queer things he brought and hear his uncouth voice and talk. They were not quite sure that my officer was not also a foreigner since he wore a uniform quite unlike the native dress. Some were so sure of it that they could not even understand him, expecting a foreign language, and commented on the similarity of American words to good Korean; 'it sounds' they said 'exactly as if he were asking us to go out and leave the great man in peace' which was precisely what he was saying to them in their own language, not in American.

We were rescued by a messenger from the bridegroom's father who asked us to come to his house, for he had dancing girls there and strolling players. Accompanied by all the villagers who were not already collected at the wedding feast (for all the world like the descriptions in the gospels), we were met on the doorsill by the father and son, with deep Korean genuflexions, and given broad sitting cushions on the polished floor, a stiff rolled cushion to lean on and each a small table piled high with food.

It has always surprised me that Griffis and Percival Lowell are so positive that there is no such a thing as a play in Korea. We had a very good play that night, so good that I brought it up to Seoul and installed it in a theatre, hoping to make a permanent thing of it and let it develop naturally to a native drama.

There were the usual tumblers in the courtyard and the dances of men and boys; the men dancing with the boys standing on their shoulders in costume, acting out the scene. Some of these are coarse, and are meant for the amusement of the mob, but as always in Korea they are rarely allowed to go too far in the presence of gentlemen. The men watch carefully for a sign of displeasure; they go as far as they dare, but at the slightest sign turn the scene to something else.

Inside the house the *kisang*, or dancing girls, went through their classic posturing in the flower dance, or the sword dance representing some very old legend, lost in the mists of time, of the attempted assassination of some great man. An enemy, not daring to attack him openly, gives a banquet and bribes a famous sword dancer to show his skill, with a real sword, meaning of course to bring about an accident. A retainer of the guest suspecting treachery but not daring to accuse so great a person as the host, takes up a sword and joins in the dance, interposing himself always with the greatest skill and grace between his master and the assassin. Both the guest and the host become aware of what is happening, but, Korean-like, are lost in admiration of the skill of the duellists who wage a deadly battle under the guise of play. Neither must permit the real object of the contest to appear, for, the principals being great gentlemen, there must be no slightest infraction of court etiquette, even in a murder. Of course the murderer sinks exhausted and the guest is saved. Korean tales always turn out the right way, for virtue is always rewarded.

Then followed the charming little play of 'Perfume of Spring,' which I set up in Seoul as the main attraction of the first Korean theatre opened by the Seoul Electric Company. It is the love story of a virtuous maid and a young student, a broken pledge ring and a long separation during which the successful student rises to the dizzy height of an imperial secret inspector, but remembers always his love for the beautiful village girl, Spring Perfume. The girl has a hard life in the meantime, for she also remembers her student. A wicked governor gives her a choice, with slavery as an alternative. The imperial inspector turns up in disguise in the nick of time, produces the all-powerful black seal of the emperor, imprisons the governor and takes over his office. He then gives the same choice to Spring Perfume, who chooses death, not recognizing him in his disguise, and he sends to her prison cell his half of their broken ring. The story is told descriptively on the stage, the actors illustrating it in pantomime accompanied by music. It was really a pretty little play and was far from being the only one in the strolling actors' repertoire. They had plenty of material for a native theatre. These plays all end virtuously, but in spite of that, our efforts to establish a place in Seoul in which they could develop naturally brought me a strong protest from conservative Korean fathers and from some missionaries in Seoul, for countenancing such depraved rascals as strolling players. Of course that was true. Korean actors were lower than they were in other parts of the East, and even the kisang, though admitted to the great houses and to the palace, was not in the least comparable to the Japanese geisha. She was not even good-looking. I never saw a Korean woman of any class who was not downright ugly. The Japanese geisha was chosen for either her intelligence or her beauty and carefully trained, not only as a dancer, but to take the place of a lady in general society. Geishas could and often did marry well. A kisang was always a sort of pariah; she could not marry anyone of consequence and was merely tolerated, half contemptuously, by the upper classes, though always treated with outward civility. The love affairs of famous geishas are among the romantic classics of Japan. No Korean of rank would imagine a love affair with a kisang. A remarkable characteristic of the geishas was their discretion. It was quite usual for politicians or business men to discuss affairs freely in their presence. I have heard serious policies of state talked over with geishas sitting there, taking no part in the conversation, but preparing pipes or cigarettes, or cups of tea or wine for the men; looking after their small creature comforts while they thrashed out things that plenty of people might have paid well to know. Discussion before geishas is as free in Japan as government and party concerns are in England in a country house over the week-end.

I always used occasions like this wedding feast to talk over Korea's affairs very loudly and publicly so that all might hear, guests, dancers, servants; so that it might be spread by the women in the inside rooms and by the gaping crowd in the courtyards, villagers and wandering actor gossips. The men were fatalistic with the weight of centuries. 'There is nothing to do about it' is as common in the Far East as in Moorish Spain: 'That which must be, will be.' I always insisted that there was a remedy, and they would answer that nobody could harm me; that my position was very different. The event proved that they were perfectly right. There was no particle of use struggling against the inertia of Korea set between the upper and the nether millstones of Japan and Russia.

I have always regretted that one spotless resting place which we did not use, for we sat as Koreans and Russians sit all night in discussion, and left with the setting of a glorious moon for our next night's destination, accompanied to the edge of the village by the musicians and a rabble of villagers, each trying to thrust himself through the crowd with some graceful phrase of farewell or good wishes for our journey; our horses well fed and fresh, our servants much the worse for wedding hospitality but happy and noisy. My companion was a man of brass and triple steel, the same who with a brother in arms had once drunk a bottle of absinthe, in liqueur glasses, without water.

Our straggling tail of musicians and shouting village people gave us something of the appearance of a widow's wedding. A village widow, in Korea, belongs to anyone who can take and keep her. Often she becomes the centre of a rough game played between villages, not for her sake, but for the sport of it.

Some group of young corner-boys, hearing of a passable widow in a village farther up the road, sets out with musicians and sling throwers to capture her. Her own people are glad enough to get rid of her, but village honour demands a fight. Sometimes it is a sham battle with a good deal of shouting and laughter. Sometimes, if there have been fatal stone fights between the two parties, it develops into a pitched battle in which the widow chattel may be roughly handled between them, like the duck in the old gaucho game of Argentina. Her lot is distinctly unhappy if one of the invaders gets a good grip on the girl and a dozen stalwart protectors have an equally good hold on the rest of her – and both sides rain down cudgel blows upon the struggling group. When the raid is purely formal and the attack and defence pre-arranged between friends and boon companions, she simply rides out of the village in a knot of shouting young fellows pretending to look fierce and followed by a jostling crowd of protectors from her own party, laughing, calling ironical farewells, while the bamboo flutes of the raiders' musicians shrill and the bagpipes squeal in triumph.

The last of our new friends dropped off at the well, set in its grove of trees, outside the last houses, where the village women come morning and evening for drinking water and gossip, and where sometimes a tiger lies hidden to seize the last girl of the long line winding up the path, each with a huge jar balanced on her head.

The songs of our caravan died down in the false dawn as we settled to the road, and once more we rode through the land of morning calm, past awakening wild things, watching us curiously and unafraid.

CHAPTER XIII

CONCESSION DIPLOMACY

THE cause of Korea's disappearance as an independent nation was land rivalry between Japan and Russia. The reason why no co-operation was possible among the other nations to prevent the issue being tried by war was the concession system of diplomacy.

European nations were still under the influence of the eighteenth-century era of territorial empire building and where they were not prepared to seize land they must at least have monopolies. If monopolies were out of the question it was necessary to create an interest in the territory of backward peoples by special concessions in one form or another.

The concession system as practised in Korea (and China) was as pernicious a form of diplomacy as any yet invented, for it hampered true business and created an artificial jealousy and hostility in the relations of all concerned.

To begin with, it was an official thing, for the legation was behind the concession from start to finish except in rare cases. A concession was in effect a business favour granted by the conceding nation to the government of the diplomat who asked for it. An immediate result of granting to one foreign nation a business favour carrying with it substantial profit to the concessionaire is to excite competition and jealousy among all other national representatives in that place. Each must succeed in wresting a similar profitable privilege from the government to which he is accredited, or the prestige of his own nation is diminished. Incidentally his own rating as an active offical may suffer at home, for failing to be as alert and skilful as his lucky or more efficient colleague.

A further result is the constant alienation of the national resources of the granting nation for the major or exclusive profit of foreigners, though some native intermediary may also be benefited, since these transactions have rarely passed without bribery in some form. A collateral result is the corruption of native officials by a friendly and presumably civilized power.

It is not to be supposed that applications for concessions were made through the legations by groups of business men wanting to place capital. More often than not the application would be made by the diplomat himself, with no capitalist in sight, on the ground that people of his nation were better at some particular thing than any others, or for the political reason that if substantial interest were granted to his nationals his government would thereby be given valid reason to keep the peace and protect the granting power.

An illustration of the official method came years after I had left Korea. I was sitting in the office of one of the law officers of the State Department. He was discussing some case with one of his subordinates and seemed to be puzzled by it. Presently I heard them mention a familiar name and suggested that I might be able to help them.

'How do you know anything about this case?' I was asked – 'it's confidential.'

'Well, I was in Korea for a long time. I happen to know that mining concession very well.'

'The devil you do! You were in Korea? What is a black seal, then?'

I explained the black seal. In Korean theory the emperor is absolute master of everything, the people, the land and everything in or under the land. All natural resources were his, all mineral wealth and particularly gold, which formed part of what the Russians, who had something of the same theory, called the imperial appanage; that is, the special property of the Crown. Even diplomacy can forget, apparently, that when the first English adventurers began the first settlements on the Atlantic coast of America, gold was stipulated as especially interesting to the Crown, and one of the great assets of the colonies was that there was not gold, so that one of the bonds fastening them to the king was loosened from the start. In Mexico, on the other hand, the need to produce gold for the Crown prevented the success of every one of the humanitarian measures the first civil viceroy and such clerics as Las Casas undertook in the interest of the native population. In Korea no signature had the slightest value without a seal, private or official, which was jealously guarded. This was so strongly established that possession of the royal great seal was evidence of legitimate succession to the throne. In order to free the emperor from the importunity of concession-hunting diplomats, some concessions were granted over the seal of the minister for foreign affairs, a decree being made legitimatizing this practice, but not making the minister's official seal exclusively valid, and it was affixed to concessions only on specific instruction or permission from the emperor himself in each individual case. The general colour of private and official seals was vermilion red.

It appeared that in this case, the ambassador at Washington of one of the great powers had attacked the validity of this gold-mining concession, a very valuable one vested in Americans, on the ground that instead of the official seal of the Korean minister of foreign affairs, it bore an 'unknown' black seal opposite an 'alleged' signature of the emperor. The ambassador, who knew Korea perfectly, proposed to secure the proper authority for the concession, provided capital of a group of his own nationals be admitted on equal terms. It seemed to me not possible that he did not know the nature of the black seal, and that he was taking a rather cynical chance on the State Department not knowing.

It was the most private and the most potent of all the imperial seals, for it conveyed the personal and indisputable will of the emperor. It was most frequently used to give power of life and death without process of law over any of his subjects, to secret inspectors whom the emperor could and sometimes did send out to unearth conspiracy or speculation among his provincial governors. Certainly it was unusual, but it was not unknown. It was the basis of half the Korean romances, for it is by the black seal that the hero is always saved. It had been affixed to this concession when the throne was tottering at the outbreak of the Russo-Japanese war, and I knew it had, for it was done in my presence to give the fullest possible security to the Americans concerned.

The Department was made up of men who had never heard of my being in Korea, so I made out an affidavit that I had been there and of the meaning of these things, and that ambassador, very well informed on the subject, dropped it completely. He, at least, knew what I was talking about.

I was told by General Legendre, but have never been able to verify it, that the emperor, worried by conflicting demands for concessions and anxious to secure some arrangement by which at least a definite revenue might be secured from natural resources if he had to alienate them, sent an officer to Levi P. Morton of all gold, copper, coal and other mines; all granite, marble and other quarries; all railway construction, all coast fisheries and all timber lands, including the famous Yalu River timber concession which last was one of the pin pricks that brought on the Russo-Japanese war. All this was to be financed and developed by solid American capitalists on a business basis, paying a definite revenue and royalties to the Crown. I was assured that the proposition had been seriously considered by Morton and only dropped because of the intervention at Washington of a European power, by whose representative it was pointed out that such a comprehensive development would amount to nothing less than a buffer between Russia and Japan (it was meant to be!) and that it might draw the United States into a position with regard to internal Korean administration which our government did not care to assume; something, perhaps in the nature of our subsequent relations in the Caribbean. Apparently our government was quite certain then that it wished to assume no such burdensome responsibility anywhere, and Mr Morton, so my informant said, went no further with it.

American business, nevertheless, had grown to be the most important in Korea, and had grown out of the usual concession beginnings. An American in Japan had come into possession of several concessions in Korea, among them one for the construction of twenty-four miles of railway from the port of Chemulpo to the capital. Navigation from the port was possible to small steamships on the Han River, but irregular because of uncharted and shifting bars, and slow since it was seventy-five miles to Seoul by river. The railway was undoubtedly important and valuable. The Japanese had been out for it. It had been granted to Americans to prevent their having it. It had drifted into the hands of this particular American, and in order not to complicate his Japanese business, he passed it on to other Americans. By them it was built and equipped very well, and in a short time, considering the constant difficulties growing out of their need to employ Japanese labour. All good clerical workers and all skilled technical labourers were Japanese. It seems hardly credible, and yet diplomacy seemed to enter even into labour relations. Wherever a work depended on Japanese it might be expected to become so difficult that sooner or later it would be sold out to them; which is exactly, what happened to this railroad. The skilled mechanics, among other discouraging habits, brought short, heavy and very effective swords with them to work, and used them to emphasize an argument on the slightest occasion. The peacemaker between them and the engineers was a giant Tennessee foreman, Phillips by name, about six feet in height. I once found him down at the bunk house knocking the head off an axe.

'The Japs are on strike again,' he said, 'I don't know what it's all about, but they've got their swords and I guess I'll have to go over and make peace; but I don't want to hurt them' – nor was he ever hurt by them. In spite of his axe helve and his terrific strength, they liked him.

Upon completion of the road it was sold to a Japanese company, to the terror and distress of the Koreans, but it could not be run as an American concern. The American concessionaires then developed the emperor's toy electric railway and made it a profitable city service. As usual, motormen, conductors and power-house engineers were Japanese, and here again the usual difficulties showed up. The line ran beautifully and was popular until a series of accidents caused serious riots. Koreans were careless. On summer nights the raised trolley bed made a pleasanter sleeping place than vermin infested huts. A green motorman taking a car out at night decapitated three before he could stop. An old man from the country, walking up the track, fascinated by the approaching car, was run down and killed. Cars were burned, the power house was attacked and the crews fled before the mob refusing to return to work unless Japanese soldiers were placed on the cars. An offer was made by Japanese capital to buy the company. This time both the Korean government and the American engineers were determined to hold on. A cable to San Francisco for a dozen power-house men and motor men who could take care of themselves under any circumtances brought out a group straight from Owen Wister's West. One of the engineers with this group came literally out of one of Owen Wister's books: he had been the telegraph operator at Separ, in the famous elocution contest.

There were two men from the Canadian Northwest Mounted Police. There was an expert bartender from an epic mining town, and a professional gambler, black hair slicked in two stiff and polished wings, and ringlets in his moustache ends. There were several cow punchers and one of the most beautifully efficient revolver shots I have ever seen. He could shoot the head off a flying bird without seeming to aim.

One day the jolly governor of Seoul, one of the American party, came to see me, much perturbed.

'I know X doesn't mean any harm,' he said, 'but he is frightening people. He shoots their top knots off as they pass along the road' (about a hundred yards' distance). He used a .45 Colt and I am quite sure it must have been disturbing. He was perfectly reasonable about it when I asked him to stop. He had only been afraid of getting out of practice. They were excellent and most entertaining men and the bartender-motorman made the most exquisite combinations Seoul had ever known. He became a feature at diplomatic parties.

The trolley line functioned smoothly again for months and then came another accident. A child running out of a blind alley was cut in two. I went down at once, after notifying the police, and found one of the Americans besieged in a switch box at Chong No. His face was a mess of blood, his nose flaattened by a stone from a Korean sling. He was about to charge a huge crowd with his Colt. I told him not to shoot; there were as many women and boys in the crowd as men. It would be just his luck to get one and make matters worse and I had sent for the police to come down at the double.

'All right, Mr Sands. What you say goes. Only, I think they ought to be killed dead, good and dead, so's they'll know they're dead and stay dead – damn 'em!'

The same man tried to get even with me for my inter-

vention on another occasion. I was in the bunk house
when a volley of stones from slings rattled in through the
windows. He seized his revolver and ran out, with me at
his heels, after a white figure disappearing up a dark alley
leading into fields. Half-way up he called suddenly
through the dark:

'Look out for the well – middle of the path.'

I jumped clear of it, and we came out in the fields, but
no Korean was in sight. He searched busily and, as I
thought, unnecessarily; I wanted to get him home
without casualties. On the way back I wondered where
the Korean had disappeared.

'Guess he's all right now – he went down that well. I
pushed him; I didn't tell you.'

We fished the man out, unconscious from terror. Fortunately it was not deep, and not enough water to
drown him.

The substitution of Americans for Japanese made it
impossible to make trouble for the company from within,
and I had been obliged, while still in the legation, to meet
more direct methods with tactics equally direct and
unblushing.

Just after the Seoul-Chemulpo railway was sold to the
Japanese company I was brought into serious conflict
with the Japanese minister, who, I strongly suspect, was
watching for a chance to bluff me, his twenty-three-year-
old colleague. The Korean minister of communications
came to me to say that he had a peremptory message from
the Japanese legation to take up the trolley tracks laid
across the right of way of the railway. I told him that I
thought it was a matter for the two companies rather than
one for the consideration of the Japanese government,
the minister of communications of Korea and me. He
tried it on, but came back again to tell me that the minister had given an ultimatum. The rails must be taken up at
once or he would send Japanese soldiers to do it. I confess
to being really disturbed – it seemed so arbitrary and out-

side of all normal diplomatic function. I realized also that it was of no use to talk to the Japanese minister. Unlike his Russian colleague who was given to bluster, Gonsuke Hayashi, was always impeccably civil, but he was also completely impervious to argument. He would smile coldly, decline to discuss and go right on his way. I asked the electric company officials to get in touch with the Japanese company at once, and at the same time asked for the loan for private purposes of my two pet crack shots, and placed them at the grade crossing with instructions that no one, in or out of uniform, was to touch the rails until I came to relieve them. I then wrote the Minister of Japan that the matter seemed to me to concern the two companies alone, and that I could only come into it in case of some act of aggression too powerful for the local authorities to give proper protection to the American company; that I had placed two men on guard and was preparing a cable to the Department to ask of the Japanese representative at Washington what reason could possibly lie for making the thing an international incident. Needless to say, the two companies came to a perfectly amicable agreement.

These anecdotes are not told in criticism of persons, but as illustrations of a system of diplomacy in which we were all involved. The Japanese bear the brunt of it here, because they were the only ones who seemed to have a definite policy. Their methods fluctuated from mild to violent according to the party in power at Tokyo; just as Hayashi Gonsuke was coldly calculating and rigidly consistent, allowing no person or thing to turn him from his path, so was his predecessor Kato Masuo, the mildest of men, too mild probably for the group to which Hayashi adhered. Every move that Hayashi made was consistent with a policy of ultimate annexation. Everything he did in his suave but icy way tended to eliminate an obstacle and I do him no wrong I think in placing him in the Miura school of politicians, with far greater intelligence and diplomatic skill than Viscount Miura. In Japan of thirty years ago, elimination of a rival or opponent was as natural and proper a thing in politics as it was in any country of Europe a few centuries ago, or as it is in Mexico to-day. We do not admit political assassination in the United States; it is a matter of custom. It is nothing derogatory to Japan or Japanese to admit that they saw nothing improper in it, under their mediaeval system, nor for many decades after the reconstruction of their national and social system. They did require that it be done according to the code. In old days a clansman who killed without witnesses was bound as a gentleman to leave some identification of himself upon the body of his victim, and that feeling still prevailed.

For some time past not only the local Japanese press, but the metropolitan and outport dailies in Japan, had been very severe with me and often violent, sometimes unscrupulous. There was more than one good reason to suppose that the local press was controlled by the legation, and I had taken up some of the rougher personal attacks with Hayashi. His assurance that Japanese officials respect the liberty of the press so meticulously that he could do nothing about it was only to be expected. Various disagreeable incidents occurred, always on the part of 'irresponsible parties,' in which equally his hands were tied, and he could do nothing. Friends among the Japanese began to warn me that an accident to me was being talked about quite openly, and that I should be careful. One day, a particular friend, the military attaché Colonel (later field marshal) Nodzu, called on me and bluntly declared he had no patience with civilian tactics, and that if ever the occasion arose when I might need refuge from irresponsible ruffians 'Japanese or any other kind,' I could find it either in his house or in that of the commander of the Japanese guard, with whom he had discussed it. In the meantime he warned me to be armed always, and particularly to sleep armed, for accidents happened more easily at night than any other time in these degenerate days. Of course I did not ask him what he meant by civilian tactics. I thought I understood that while he did not object to the elimination of an opponent he still believed in leaving behind some mark of identification, as a gentleman should. I took his intimation as perfectly natural and completely part of the diplomacy of the day; Japan had a definite policy and meant that nothing should stand in the way of it. If it was a concession or a company or any other business entity it must be acquired or controlled by Japanese capital. If that could not be done immediately, any business to which Japanese employees were necessary must be so disturbed that sooner or later the owners would be glad to sell. If it was an individual who stood in the way, he must be got out of the way. It was only the business policy of Europe as understood by keen Japanese observers of Western practice and applied with that meticulous care for detail which is characteristic of them. Policy would be elaborated to the last degree, and certainly my position in Korea must enter into it.

The Japanese passion for detail during their construction period sometimes had strange repercussions in police regulations, bewildering or irritating, as one happened to fall within their working. At the time of official mourning for the dowager express of Japan a circular came from the grand master of ceremonies to every legation in Tokyo describing the etiquette to be observed, based, of course, upon the rigid age-old formulas of the course, and the custom of observing mourning for parents and royalty for years at a time. Among many other things, exact instructions covered such minutiae as the stud and cuff links of men and the Victorian mysteries of women's inner dress. Simultaneously a police regulation was issued forbidding music, noise, disorder, rioting and conflagrations during the whole mourning period. Of course the legations observed their own national etiquette in such matters, and the rest of the foreign colony observed none at all, while the Japanese people struggled with the intricacies of their particular problem. Naturally native officialdom and native people were annoyed by the refusal of foreigners to pay what they considered proper respect to imperial memory.

In Korea, during a temporary Japanese occupation, voluminous sumptuary laws were issued in which the careful drafter found place for the number of dishes a Korean might have on his table at each meal, and the number and quality of clothes he might wear, according to his station in life; pipe stems over twelve inches in length were forbidden (Koreans liked reed pipe stems like 'church wardens' thirty-six inches long) and halters for led animals might not exceed three feet in length. There was a basis of sense at the bottom of each of these absurdities, but they could no more be enforced than prohibition upon an unwilling people and did more to make public feeling sharp and even hostile than much more serious political blunders.

Translated into diplomacy such a passion for detail made war inevitable, and translated into military strategy and tactics, as it was, it only made the Manchurian campaign a deadlock, loosed in victory by Roosevelt's intervention. Thirty years ago, the Japanese were using tools and weapons that they did not fully know. To-day they use them as their own, backed by all their own inherent skill and art.

CHAPTER XIV

FOREIGN POLICY

IF the Japanese seemed to have a policy, definite down to the last detail, hard and hand polished, Russian diplomacy seemed as inchoate as the American and even less tangible than that, for at least John Hay's mind was rigidly made up that under no circumstances should the United States get into trouble in the Far East. That was something anyhow, even if negative. One could never be sure that the Russian enigma had anything so definite as a negation in sight. Nobody knew which of the things Russian diplomats did were devilishly subtle and which were simply inept and meaningless, with no relation to anything. We all thought they must mean something. Russia was so big and mysterious and aloof. It is a great asset to a conspirator nation to have a language so remote from all other human sounds that you could make a handy list of all foreigners who speak and understand it. The Russians themselves seemed so different from the rest of mankind. They were so shameless in their infractions of other people's conventions about fair play, or graft and all the other little rules that make up the game of society. They were so unpredictable; so brilliant and such clods; so full of vague philosophies, of poetry, of the literature of Europe; so disdainful – and ignorant – of the principles upon which other, slow thinking people had built up the system to which they held. They were such perfect linguists and so witty; or so completely impervious to any Western thought and so completely Oriental that one began to understand how easily China might absorb into the Russian Empire. One never felt that one knew anything at all about Russia and the Russians; one felt oppressed by their colossal weight and could understand what must be the Japanese state of mind confronted by it, menaced by it, without knowing exactly in what the menace might consist. Even those Westerners who did not like or trust Japan thrilled in admiration when Japan determined to see what this ogre was made of, and whether it had flesh and bone and blood like plain humans, and the sons of Japanese clansmen fitted their fathers' heavy two-handed samurai blades to modern sabre hilts. Ossendowski's recent descriptions of his life in Russia seem so fantastic to many people that they simply reject them. Anyone who knows Russia even on the surface, nevertheless recognizes those descriptions as accurate. No one would question German courage or French courage or English courage. Russian courage, with everything else that concerned the Russians, was a riddle. The Russian soldier was completely insensible, apparently, to fear or pain. The Russian officers we saw on the frontiers were often completely moral cowards and yet fatalistically indifferent to death. Many of these officers were men who had been exiled to garrison duty or other service in Siberia and the border lands. Such games as hide and seek in a dark room, the players on one side and a blindfolded man with a revolver on the other, were common enough among officers to whom Siberia was as heavy an exile as it was to the convict for life. They really played that game, shooting at the sound of a voice or a bell, the bell holder, if he survived, taking the revolver in his turn. They played it in the same cynically fatalistic spirit as that in which a bored Cossack officer in one of these small posts, arguing that no one could die until his time came, put his service revolver to his head and pulled the trigger. The cartridge failed to explode, but on going out from there he was killed by a drunken convict.

There was that kind of courage among them, plenty of

it; but it seemed to me that it was the dubious courage of the suicide, rather than the serene determination of him 'whose head is bloody, but unbowed.' Everywhere we saw brilliant, cynical grafters, men who played so fast and loose with all things our slower minds respected that we believed the whole Russian organism must feel frightfully secure in its unprincipled strength, just as, less than two decades later, a much wider audience felt about the Bolsheviks. One felt that it must mean something, and that something loomed unknowable and sinister.

It was not till I went through those last days of the Romanoff dynasty which Maurice Paléologue describes, and through the succeeding revolutions which he did not see, listened every evening to Lenin's glacial oratory and watched him and Trotzky consolidate the Bolshevik power, that I came to the conclusion that 'Russia' does not mean anything at all, and never did. 'Russia' means whatever handful of men holds the reins and the knout at the same time. It does not matter in the least whether it is an emperor or a commissar. There never was a truer word about it than the witty French aphorism: '*Le trône de Russie n'est ni héréditaire ni électif; il est occupatif.*' Whoever held the reins and knout was Russia: whoever occupied the attention of the occupant of the throne formed Russian policy. What was true then is true to-day, but we are only beginning to know it. It has taken a long time to piece the Russian mystery.

I think we did not realize either what a conglomerate the Russians were. We thought of Russians as Russians. It did not occur to us then that M. Speyer and M. Waeber or Russian diplomats and officers with Polish names acted quite differently from diplomats and officers with names Russian, Tartar, Kalmuck or Georgian.

Whatever we may write in retrospect to prove our own diplomatic omniscience, I at least never met nor heard of any one thirty years ago, who realized that the vagaries of Russian diplomacy were not connected by any con-

tinuous conscious policy, and that they certainly were
affected by the nationality of the particular Russian
diplomat concerned; it made a great difference whether
he were a Baltic baron, a Russian, a Cossack, or a Tartar.
All were Russians but all made up their own communities
and held to their own code of conduct. They even made
up regiments in the army from their own communities
speaking the same language. Even Americans then did
not realize how similar the Russian composition might be
to modern America. Pavlow, in Korea's last days, was
temperamentally stormy or wily by turns, arrogant and
domineering or overwhelmingly friendly; a lump of sugar
in one hand, the bit and bridle in the other. No one knew
that there was nothing underneath. Perhaps the Japanese
had guessed it, but Japanese have not yet taken to writing
memoirs in the indiscreet Western style, and telling what
they knew and thought or did not know.

Hayashi Gonsuke, sphinx-like, inscrutable, impec-
cable, but icily courteous, rarely failed in the severely
correct attitude. When he did he made haste to remedy it
openly. Underneath, however, he was aggressive and pro-
vocative, not haphazard, but each move marked out in
advance and intentional. He was either the most imper-
sonally perfect public servant and party man that ever
was, or he was what I think he was: a convinced annexationist himself, hardening a party sentiment at home
to a definite war policy. I doubt that he was anybody's
tool. I think that he saw no way out of the Korean *impasse*
but war; that he did not believe co-operation among the
powers possible under the existing trend of diplomacy;
that, in consequence, neutralization of Korea could not
lead to any satisfactory result, but would only leave
Korea free to sink still lower in the morass of official
incompetence. I believe also that he felt Korea to be
economically essential to Japan's development, while to
permit Russia to dominate Korea, or to agree, as Pavlow
suggested, to a division of Korea would simply mean the

erection that much nearer to Japan of an unscrupulous
and irresponsible power that would have to be fought
anyway sooner or later. There were strong differences of
opinion about the Korean situation among the Tokyo
statesmen. I may be entirely wrong, but I attribute to
Hayashi Gonsuke the gradual hardening of the war party
and the development of a consistent policy in that direction. At any rate that is what his every act looked like.
Viscount Miura resorted to open and official violence to
remove obstacles from his path, involving the whole
government and nation in his acts. Hayashi had infinitely
greater tact and patience. He, too, intended that there
should be no obstacles in the way, but it was his policy to
remove them at night, a little at a time as long as time permitted. Miura was of the school of the Russian Hitrovo
who could bomb a whole Balkan cabinet out of his way
and be damned to public opinion. Hayashi permitted
obstacles no more than Miura and Hitrovo, but he carefully prepared public opinion in favour of the result he
wanted and allowed no false step, or retrieved it quickly,
if it turned out that way. I could play at diplomacy with
the Russian group; I could not take liberties with
Hayashi. This picture of him grew to be a conviction in
the five years during which I faced him. In no other way
could I explain the consistent opposition to every reform
I attempted. Reform raised an obstacle in the way of
annexation. there was no other explanation of the presence of Japanese so frequently in major disorders in the
provinces, for Japanese are peaceful people. They do not
develop adventurous individuals, soldiers of fortune as
we do. The Ronin, the masterless man of the old days of
clan chivalry, or the soshi, the turbulent and irresponsible tool of more recent Japanese politics do correspond
somewhat to that type; but in the case of the classic Ronin
it was a high ideal that moved him– in the case of the soshi
it was bread and butter. In neither was it the pure spirit of
adventure. When Japanese turned up as consistent

troublemakers one could legitimately suspect a master mind. They were not that way by nature. They are essentially courteous people; violent and discourteous personal attacks in their newspapers could reasonably be set down as inspired by authority. They are orderly and friendly people. They can and do have their personal quarrels, but not with strangers. When a Japanese goes out of his way in an orderly community to quarrel with or offer violence to a stranger it is safe to assume that there is a motive behind it which is not personal. When that attitude extends to a person in public life, one may be quite certain that it is political and that at least as much has been intimated by someone higher up, as in the case of Thomas à Becket. The constant drive against the development of any foreign business that might constitute an interest to be protected; the thousand and one petty intrigues against the most obviously non-political business; the impossibility of employing the only skilled labour there was, Japanese, in any business without totally unwarranted trouble and disorder, followed inevitably by protective intervention by their legation; the consistent acquisition of land outside of the legal territory by bank crop liens, foreclosed mortgages on loans at twelve per cent. per month; the notorious lending of bribe money in large sums to Korean candidates for provincial office, with a first lien on the taxes to be collected in that district, and its consequent confirmation of the corruption and bribery we all deplored officially, seemed to point in every case to a political end. Irresponsible taxation was the principal source of disorder and rebellion in the provinces. If Hayashi did not know that, he knew less than anybody else in Korea, which is not at all likely. He could have discountenanced Japanese participation in that particular and notorious industry. I never heard that he did, and taking all these things together, it seemed the most natural thing in the world that he should not, for he was the only one who had a definite policy, shaped down to the last detail.

The average Japanese is respectful of authority and intensely patriotic. He is quite human, however; he has his own opinions. He is not separated from other men by any such fictitious chasm as it was the fashion to believe. He can and does have friendships with Western individuals and he can and does discuss these things. There was a divergence of private opinion among Japanese, though cautiously expressed, about policy in Korea. The notable thing about it was that Japanese policy could not be discussed with Japanese officials. I never got a hearing for my own opinions except from one, Prince Hirobumi Ito. Some were gently deprecatory of allusion to the situation in Korea, most became something more than reserved when the subject was raised. With Hayashi I could never even approach the subject.

That did not mean that there was any personal hostility between me and the Japanese legation. On the contrary, I had cordial friendships among its members. Hayashi was scrupulously polite always. Eki Hioki, then secretary and later minister to Peking, was invariably friendly. Akidzuki, the head of the consular establishment, was a charming companion, as was Field Marshal Nodzu and the military contingent. The junior members, Midzuno, Shinobu and the baby of the legation, Haniwara (so popular in later years in Washington) who rose to be ambassador to the United States and vice minister of foreign affairs, were all members of the same intimate circle. I am convinced that there never was anywhere among Japanese the slightest personal hostility to me, in spite of the rather disreputable newspaper campaign carried on against me. There was a definite policy. Everything I did affected that policy in some way. I could not be allowed to win, and there could be no sentiment about it. I stood in the very centre of what was hardening into a life or death national struggle. Everything I did had significance. When the Boxer war broke out in China, Korea could have been led to follow suit. The slightest move in that direction would have been followed by Japanese military occupation, with full approval of the allies, and Russia could not have objected for the moment. The raids from Manchuria over our border were equally satisfactory from the point of view of annexationist policy. If they continued, Japan might use them as an occasion to preserve order; if in attempting to stop them I raised a storm along the frontier, the result would be the same. An occasional push or dexterous touch by Hayashi here and there was all that was needed to keep the situation in his hand. There was no diplomat in Seoul who was a match for him, for he knew what he was doing, and no one else did.

CHAPTER XV

THE END

A S far as administrative reforms are concerned, there is not much to which I can point with pride. I did not succeed in five years in abolishing official bribery, nor in training up a body of officials capable of even that minimum of justice and common sense that would have been enough for the administration of the peaceful and easy-going people in the provinces. I never succeeded in establishing co-ordination among the various foreign schools that would have formed a nucleus for such a body of rural administrators; and my plan for neutralization of Korea in case of a Far Eastern conflict by what has come to be called in our day multilateral peace treaties was sunk without trace, completely *spurlos*, when, proposing to attach myself to the special mission I was sending to London for the Queen's Jubilee, I was politely but firmly requested by Sir John Jordan to substitute for myself the British consul at Chemulpo, and given to understand that this arrangement would be more acceptable to Her Majesty's government. I did not dare entrust the discussion of such a subject to a perfectly inexperienced Korean prince who was head of the mission. I believed I knew Englishmen well enough to know that it would be possible for me to get a hearing for my ideas, even if their hands were bound by the treaty with Japan. I could not get my plans before our own people through Washington; nobody in the Seoul legations was receptive, and I felt that I could not force the issue of my going to London in the face of the British consul general's plain request that I stay away. I never got a full and intelligent hearing anywhere but in the quarter where I had the least right to expect it: in Japan, and from Prince Ito who became resident general and practical ruler of Korea after the military occupation.

Of course I had urged my simple plan upon the emperor frequently and at length. He always listened courteously and trustingly, but the poor man never had the first glimmering of what it was all about. The sum of his philosophy was that he was the master of his people and what was theirs was his. Moreover, communication at best was complicated and difficult because he could not be left alone by his attendants. Behind the scenes of even the most private audience with any foreigner there were eager ears stretched to hear what was said, and, half heard, it was sure to be twisted when it was discussed with his confidants afterward. Like some of the romantic Valois, he was not always, or even frequently, open to matters of State. They bored him; though he was always frankly ashamed when he was forced to stifle a tiny yawn behind a delicate ivory hand, and apologized eagerly by saying that he had slept badly. Four long intervals of a hundred days each gave the court flatterers and those who did not want me there ample opportunity to break down any impression I was able to make. On each of those occasions I had notoriously seen death, and on many others besides, but I had not published it. Court etiquette was rigid and made no exceptions. Anyone who had seen death as I had on the Yalu, at Quelpaert, in the cholera epidemic and in street riots, must not come near the emperor for one hundred days, an ancient ceremonial which no emergency could change.

I was on duty at the palace when Prince Ito came over with certain confidential plans from Tokyo for the emperor's consideration. They came to my ears promptly and I agreed with a large part of what I heard, though I was not absolutely sure that much of it was not distorted in transmission. I found it so difficult to comment on them third-hand that I decided to go and see him, in spite of the barriers thrown around him; we might be able to work on the same side.

I found him in a tea house, alone except for a group of the best geisha the Japanese town could produce, in most jovial mood and flushed with sake. To my astonishment, I interrupted the great statesman in a song, a frivolous song, and to his astonishment I told him that I had heard the substance of his very secret interview with the emperor and wanted to be quite sure of what he had actually said, or, as in the simplicity of my heart I told him, I would not know how to advise.

Hirobumi Ito was one of the greatest statesmen in Japan and certainly one of the great men of his time, but it seemed to me that he had not forgotten the simplicity of his obscure origin. It was unquestionably a shock to be invaded in his privacy. It was a shock to be caught in wine and singing, and by one who was commonly accepted in Japanese official circles as an enemy of Japanese policy. It was a final and complete blow to be told that such a person would like to know the full content of a private message from one emperor to another, in order to be able to judge between them. I waited for the inevitable stroke of apoplexy, but it did not come. Instead he asked me to sit down, offered me a cup of native wine and suggested that we talk it out. I have no idea what Prince Ito's recommendations may have been to his own government with regard to Korea. I am quite sure, however, that he could listen to the opinion of others and that he could have inaugurated a better system of government. The worst thing Koreans ever did for themselves was to assassinate him and kill Durham White Stevens my successor. What I gathered from the emperor and the babble of eunuchs as well as the bits that had been pieced together by intelligent men and earnest patriots like Min Yong Whan, pointed in the direction of a proposal by Prince Ito, sanctioned by the emperor of Japan, to form a close

alliance between Japan, China, and Korea. It seemed to
mean a union of the Far East, possibly a federation in
which Japan having been more successful than the others
in assimilating Western knowlege, should guide them
both in general policy and in practical Western training.
Ito neither confirmed nor denied my understanding of
his mission; he could not, since it was confidential. The
striking thing about him was that he consented to discuss
the major policies of his country at all, and with a very
young American greenhorn whom chance had thrown
into the position of trying single-handed to hold apart the
two great empires of the East. It was a fantastic position,
and perhaps that very fact appealed to the great man Ito
was. He pointed out the utter impossibility of my own
situation, agreed cordially and kindly with everything I
had tried to do, insisting, however, on the insuperable
obstacles I realized only too well, from living with them
day by day and every night. He encouraged me to speculate upon hypothetical federation of the three Oriental
empires: Japan, China and Korea. I thought it possible
and that a sufficient number of the Western powers
might be brought to agreement, provided he could create
confidence in the Chinese and Koreans. The terrible
devastation of the latter in the sixteenth century by
Japanese armies was still a Korean memory, but not so
strong, in my opinion, that it could not have been lived
down. The over-rigid sumptuary laws imposed by a
Japanese bureaucracy and affecting every part of Korean
private life had harmed the influence of Japan during one
brief period when they were in power in the peninsula.
Then the Miura regime and the ruthless murder of the
queen, while it had terrified the Koreans so that they
could deny nothing to the Japanese, had certianly not
created an atmospere of trust. With terror went also deep
hatred, and hatred had not been diminished nor confidence restored by the icy administration of Hayashi
Gonsuke. A union or federation would have to take into

serious consideration those very hard facts about Korea. Concerning China I could not even speculate, for theirs was an older culture than Japan's and a proud one. I was not sure that China was greatly impressed by Japan's acquisition of Western applied science, or had even begun to believe that the Middle Kingdom was not able to handle single-handed and in its own way the rest of all the world, Japan included. As for the Western European powers, there was the concession diplomacy and the growing system of spheres of influence. Would a federation under the hegemony of Japan strike them, rather, as a monopoly by Japan of those highly competitive things? Could sufficient assurance be given to the United States that trade doors would not be closed against them in the Far Eastern markets? A real federation might work. A super-Boxer movement, that is, an anti-foreign alliance of the three empires, could not work except by force, and I made a bold plea for my own favourite child, the neutralization of Korea by absolute peace treaties with every major power, as a first step toward an atmosphere of confidence preparatory to a Far Eastern union. I can only say that Prince Ito was serious and receptive, as he sat there on the floor of the tea house, a little elderly man, stroking his thin grey beard as he listened, kindly and attentive, or talked with excellent knowledge of Korean conditions, as if I were really a power there and not the adventurer in diplomacy the local press considered me to be, whom the Japanese government would sweep away or crush when its patience was exhausted. I left him with the deep satisfaction of having been heard by an intelligent man with sympathy, and of having put Korea's case and my own before the leading statesman of Japan. Nothing tangible came of it.

In another interval of enforced exclusion from the palace I went up to Peking, to establish a Korean mission there and to learn at first-hand conditions subsequent to the defeat of the Boxers and the taking of Peking by the allied troops. When I returned, I found that in spite of the definite terms of my contract a Belgian adviser had been appointed in my place by Ye Yong Ik with the support of the Russians and the French. Since it was an accomplished fact and people had understood by now that no nine cruisers would gather in the port of Chemulpo, as they had for McLeavy Brown on a similar occasion, the Belgian minister was not in the least interested in what my own contract specified. Ye Yong Ik, the Peng Yang ruffian miner who had saved the queen, had become a power in the palace, with the aid of the Lady Om, ex-kitchenmaid. No one quite knew who stood behind him, for he seemed to be equally in favour with Pavlow and Hayashi. Probably both used him, and even more probably he used them, and tried the risky game of playing them against each other. There was no reason for him to be hostile to me, for he had been a frequent visitor, and I had always treated him well. Hostility showed quickly nevertheless, for as guardian of the imperial purse and keeper of the emperor's seal he cut off my salary and requisitioned my house. I could have resigned, but the climax seemed too near to leave then, nor was I so sure that the emperor knew anything about it.

The Japanese were becoming agitated over the rumoured appearance of Cossacks on the Yalu. Cossacks can be anything; regular troops or hired concession police. They might be imperial guardsmen or private servants and retainers. The Cossack is a free man; his own tribal dress is his uniform, his horse and rifle are his own. Whether he serves you, serves as a trooper in the army or lives at home, half farmer and half cowboy, his dress and arms and all equipment are the same.

A mysterious group of grand dukes of Russia and notorious speculators had obtained a timber concession on the upper Yalu, the same that had been offered years before to Levi P. Morton. A member of a great Jewish family, famous international financiers, offered me my own price to find out what the Japanese meant to do about it. I wanted badly to know what they both meant to do about it, and exactly what it was the Russians were doing, but I was tied. I could not go again to the border to look for Cossacks or for grand dukes.

Anyone could know that the Japanese were alarmed and angry. Anyone could know that they would not tolerate a Russian advance into Korea, but nobody in our part of the world knew whether Russia was in the hands of irresponsible people (we know now that she was) or dominated by a clear and considered determination to annex Korea and try conclusions with Japan and England. Adam Zad was simply a great mysterious, threatening bulk that nobody understood. Every move anybody made began to wear the meaning of a manoeuvre on the chessboard of war.

In the first days of February, 1904, the wardroom officers of the cruiser *Variag* asked several of us to lunch. I was late starting for the port, and presently I had a telephone call from Chemulpo from one of the party who had gone ahead. The executive officer of the *Variag*, he reported, had come ashore to call off the lunch and pay up all the ship's bills and to say good-bye. Men crowded around him at the club, all keyed for any event, to ask him what was happening.

'Look out and see!' he laughed.

Beyond Roze Island, which divided the two inlets of Chemulpo Harbour, lay a half circle of slender destroyers; beyond them, again, a formation of light cruisers, bending out of sight beyond the headland, and on the horizon the heavy smoke columns of the Japanese grand fleet.

'What is it all about?'

'We don't know. They have not declared war that anyone knows, but an hour ago we had a message to surrender.'

'What are you going to do?'

'We can't be the first Europeans to surrender to an Asiatic fleet. We are going to try and break through to Port Arthur. We haven't a chance. Goodbye!'

The next train to the port took everybody who could move, for what was happening was in the harbour itself, almost in the very town. Sure enough, across the only channel that would clear the *Variag* at that tide lay a cruiser, about her weight in gunfire, several light vessels hovered a little farther out and the rest had drawn farther to sea. It was to be a duel, and they meant to give the *Variag* a fighting chance. Within the harbour lay an American cruiser, an English cruiser and a Frenchman. Slowly the *Variag* got under way followed by the station-naire gunboat, *Koreetz*, and a Russian mail steamer. She passed out of the harbour in a long sweep, and hardly through the channel, certainly within three miles of the shore line, engaged the cruiser and both disappeared around a corner, followed by the light fleet. In the distance the great battleships and heavy cruisers kept the lists, contemptuous of what was happening inside.

After an interval of heavy gunfire, back they all came into the harbour, the *Variag* very slowly, heeled over in a heavy list, nd took up her anchorage again, a shattered wreck, and again a cruiser barred the entrance channel, like a sentry. The *Koreetz* did not show damage at that distance. Boats and launches went busily between the Russian ships and the foreign cruisers. Just at lunch time the *Koreetz* blew up in a tall column of heavy smoke, raining burnt photographs, charred playing cards and steel all over the town. A little later the *Variag* sank. Our friend, the executive officer, had been on the bridge when she went out. The place where he was standing was struck by the first heavy shell.

Then came a rushing destroyer into the harbour, and once more boats plied busily between her and the French and British cruisers. Finally, an English officer and one of our own came up to the club and it was possible to get the news. The Russian ships had made a good try. When they came back, all living men from both were removed to the French and British cruisers, ours remaining neutral. The French, of course, took all they could, as Russia's ally; but Japan's ally, the Englishman, took all the rest, out of which grew a complication. The little destroyer had brought in a peremptory message to both to give up the Russians as prisoners of war. Both refused. According to our informant another message stated that, if refused, the Russians would be taken. The English captain's answer was:

'Ally or no ally, people aren't taken from English ships!' And he stripped for action – which reminded me somewhat of the war of 1812. Nothing happened, but much later I heard it gossiped that he had been officially reprimanded for the sharpness of his reply and privately commended for making it, as one does in the navy. Everyone thought for a time that there would be another fight right there, for in streamed ship after ship toward the harbour. They were the convoy of troopships. Lighters and coolies appeared by magic. Troops, each in its complete unit, landed like clockwork and marched off toward the north. Not even the great fighting machine that impressed observers so deeply with its crushing strength as it passed through Belgium ten years later was more precise or more superbly handled than the Japanese army of occupation of 1904. They were magnificent troops. I had seen the Kaiser lead his grand manoeuvres and I have seen the armies of the World War, but there was never anything finer than that landing. With Japanese one does not expect disorder; they are not only disciplined, but self-disciplined, people. What struck everyone was their courtesy and consideration in their contacts with the natives.

In the next few days it was arranged for Pavlow, his household, his official family and the whole Russian colony to go aboard the French cruiser. A special train took them to the port, with all honours, high Japanese officers escorting them. The British cruiser bore away its part of the survivors of the *Variag* and *Korretz* for internment in some British colony. My turn should come next, and I waited with considerable curiosity.

Since everybody knew that Ye Yong Ik had excluded me by the simple process of stopping my pay and negotiating for a Belgian to take my place, and that our legation had acquiesced in the breach of contract, the Japanese might have simply ignored me, but they were conducting their first war with Europe in knightly fahsion.

Eki Hioki, later minister to China, bore the message, which was simple.

'I am instructed,' he said, 'to invite you to join Prince Ito in the temporary administration which is to be established here.'

I think that there was no one with whom I would rather have been associated in high politics than Prince Ito. I was enormously flattered and appreciated what was a real compliment, but I had been opposing their policies for four years. I told Hioki so and asked him what he would think of me if I flopped to the winning side even if my own had gone back on me.

'We know that, but we do want you.'

'Could you think well of me if I did, Hioki?'

'You are asking me a private question and this is official.'

'The alternative?'

'A bad one, I am afraid. I am sorry. There is a cavalry transport leaving at once. I can't even tell you where she is going, but only that I will see to your things myself and put them on the American collier in Chemulpo. Of course you will be treated with every consideration and transferred to the first vessel going to America.'

No one could have been more amiable than the captain of the transport. He had the air of one hugging a gigantic thrill. As we ran down the coast toward Masampho, he asked me to go below decks and keep out of sight.

'I can't ask you to keep away from portholes,' he said with a grin, 'but do please keep out of sight. I have to run into a harbour along here with dispatches.'

He had good reason to keep me out of sight. Cable dispatches had told the world of the first naval attack on Port Arthur and how the Russian forts had been knocked about with practically no damage to the attacking fleet. That was news of great value to the navies of the world. Here was the fleet itself, tucked away in a Korean bay, battered, bruised and badly smashed, as one would expect it to be after engaging powerful land batteries. It was in no condition to be seen by foreigners. Thousands of workmen were furiously repairing huge holes. Dry docks had been towed over from Japan. I wondered how they had kept their activities so secret and whether it was some suspicion of their preparations here which had caused the Russian offer to me to find out. For a long time past we had been aware of a particular interest in this harbour. Various attempts had been made to get it in concession. No doubt the whole place had been surveyed and blueprinted, but this whole busy world of people and equipment for repair must have come out with the fleet, been set up and prepared for the result of the great sea attack on what Admiral Dubassoff thought he had made an impregnable fortress. I rather think he had, in spite of the result. Admiral Dubassoff was utterly opposed to war with Japan, but he was a competent sailor, an able administrator and glaringly honest in these sordid pre-war surroundings. Under him Port Arthur might have told a different story than it did under the incompetent wastrel Alexeieff – for the most impregnable fortress in the world depends on its defenders. I made as good use as I could of our short stop, for I realized that there were no foreign observers with the fleet and all the war correspondents were held up in Japan or corralled in Seoul.

My captain landed me in Nagasaki, where I found the *Thomas*, army transport, en route from Manila to San Francisco and threw myself on the tender mercies of a quartermaster captain who did not like civilians. I got passage only by insistence that I must get through at once to President Roosevelt, and was quartered with the negro non-commissioned officers of the twenty-fourth infantry. With rare tact the coloured sergeants made me comfortable since I was forbidden the officers' deck. They got me such little luxuries as personal towels and soap, the best ventilated space in their sleeping quarters and as much privacy as was possible. Their manners were perfect and their unobtrusive attentions delicate.

Straight through to Washington, as fast as steam could carry me, and to the White House. Roosevelt was incredulous. What I told him did not tally with what he heard from Tokyo. My story of the grand fleet was simply not possible. It contradicted every report he had. I was flying in the face of facts! – and so for everything else I had to tell him about the East. It was all rather disheartening.

That night I was dining with Justice Oliver Wendell Holmes. He had a British major-general who had just come from India by way of the Far East. Over the coffee I asked him as questions the things I had told Roosevelt that morning, and found that he agreed with what I had said.

'I wish you would tell our President what you have just told us,' I said.

'No need! Your President is a remarkably well-informed man. I had a long talk with him this afternoon, and, would you believe it? He actually knew the condition of the Japanese fleet. I don't suppose there is another man in America who knows where that fleet is!'

The State Department was not interested either. Everybody there, including all who had never been in the

East knew so much more than I did that I felt very small, and decided never to speak of it again.

After several months I was sent for by Mr Taft, Secretary of War, but holding down the lid of the whole government, for President and Secretary of State were absent. Mr Taft had a problem in Panama. Gen. George Davis, governor of the Canal Zone, and John Barrett, minister to Panama, were at loggerheads, and each was right. The minister insisted that communications to the Panama government must go through the legation, while the governor insisted that without the privilege of going direct in canal matters, the canal could not be built. Taft wanted to withdraw both and combine both offices in one man. Panama, likely to be very susceptible in its new independence, might quite easily see in such an arrangement the beginning of imperialistic annexation. Did I want to try my hand at a delicate negotiation, not at all likely to succeed, and get Charles E. Magoon accepted for the two posts of governor and minister? I did, and so found myself back in the regular service, my adventure finished.

I rolled up the map of the Far East and turned to learning Latin America.